"Jimmy Evans has a way of combining Scripture with honest stories about his own marriage to show that no relationship is beyond God's help. *Lifelong Love Affair* is insightful, moving, challenging, and so entertaining. This book is full of wisdom."

—**Dr. Gary Smalley**, author of *The DNA of Relationships* and *I Promise*

"God has a plan for your marriage, and it includes passion, romance, fun, and (shh!) a fulfilling sex life. Jimmy Evans is a leading voice in making sure husbands and wives are aware of God's plan for them. If you're married or even thinking about getting married, read this book. Now."

—**Christine Caine**, director of Equip and Empower Ministries; founder of The A21 Campaign

"Jimmy Evans isn't just one of the best speakers and authors on marriage, he's also a close personal friend. I know that what he shares in *Lifelong Love Affair* comes from his heart and from the incredible insight and revelation he has received from the Lord. Apply these biblical principles, and you'll have more than a good marriage—you'll build a strong, lasting marriage, rooted in God's eternal love."

—**Robert Morris**, senior pastor, Gateway Church; bestselling author of *The Blessed Life*, *From Dream to Destiny*, and *The God I Never Knew*

"Whether speaking from his own experience or relating powerful insights from Scripture, Jimmy Evans provides married couples the tools and inspiration to make their relationship last forever. If you want an indestructible marriage, reading this is step one."

—**Chris Hodges**, pastor, Church of the Highlands, Birmingham, Alabama; author of *Fresh Air*

Lifelong
LOVE
AFFAIR

Lifelong
LOVE
AFFAIR

How to Have a Passionate and
Deeply Rewarding Marriage

Jimmy Evans
with Frank Martin

BakerBooks
a division of Baker Publishing Group
Grand Rapids, Michigan

© 2012 by Jimmy Evans

Published by Baker Books
a division of Baker Publishing Group
P.O. Box 6287, Grand Rapids, MI 49516-6287
www.bakerbooks.com

Printed in the United States of America

Library of Congress Cataloging-in-Publication Data

Evans, Jimmy.
    Lifelong love affair : how to have a passionate and deeply rewarding marriage / Jimmy Evans with Frank Martin.
        p.   cm.
    ISBN 978-0-8010-1478-9 (cloth)
    ISBN 978-0-8010-1541-0 (international trade paper)
    1. Marriage—Religious aspects—Christianity. I. Martin, Frank, 1958– II. Title
BV835.E875 2012
248.8′44—dc23   2012010198

The author is represented by the literary agency of Alive Communications, Inc., 7680 Goddard Street, Suite 200, Colorado Springs, CO 80920. www.alivecommunications.com

To protect the privacy of those who have shared their stories with the author, some details and names have been changed.

The internet addresses, email addresses, and phone numbers in this book are accurate at the time of publication. They are provided as a resource. Baker Publishing Group does not endorse them or vouch for their content or permanence.

13   14   15   16   17   18   7   6   5   4   3   2

To my precious grandson,
Reed Henry Evans.
You bring such joy to our hearts.
May your future be full of blessings and happiness.
And may you and your generation take the land for God.

Contents

Foreword

A Hollywood screenwriter comes home to find his house burned to the ground. His wife, sobbing, says, "Oh, John, it was awful. I was cooking and the phone rang. It was your agent. We were talking, and I didn't see the stove was on fire. The flames were unbelievable. It went up so quickly. We're wiped out, honey—destroyed. There's nothing left. But thank God, little Fluffy and I escaped by the skin of—"

"Whoa—wait just a minute. Back up," John says. "Did you say my agent called?"

We must confess that we felt a bit like that writer when Jimmy Evans called. Not that our house was on fire, thankfully. But learning that Jimmy was about to publish a new marriage book grabbed our attention. Why? Because we knew that in spite of all the urgent demands that have a way of burning up our schedules, we needed to set them all aside and read *Lifelong Love Affair*.

So we did. And our marriage is stronger for it.

We first met Jimmy more than a decade ago when he invited us to conduct a marriage seminar at his amazing church in Amarillo, Texas. But even before that, we knew Jimmy by reputation. Everyone who knows Jimmy from his books, television broadcast, website, preaching, or live seminars knows just how passionate he is when it comes to helping couples build rock-solid marriages (not to mention his own marriage to Karen). In fact, you'll be hard-pressed to find someone who is more dedicated to giving couples practical tools for

11

lifelong love. And that's why we were so thrilled by the opportunity to get a sneak peek at this wonderful book.

Lifelong Love Affair takes God's timeless principles and shows everyday couples how to put them to work. It unpacks the eternal truths of Scripture and shows us how to live them out in one of the most challenging yet rewarding relationships God has given us: marriage. Not so that our relationships will simply survive but so they will stand strong and flourish in spite of the proverbial floods and fires trying to destroy them.

And know this: Jimmy is not in the business of giving out glib platitudes about lifelong love. Nope. He cuts to the heart of the matter and shows us how to make our married love affair nothing short of certifiably indestructible.

Drs. Les and Leslie Parrott
www.LesandLeslie.com

Acknowledgments

First and foremost I want to thank my incredible wife, Karen, for everything she does for me and our ministry to marriages. This book is as much hers as it is mine. Everything I write and teach flows from the sharing of our lives. I could not have done this without the continual investment of her love, patience, wisdom, and sacrifice.

I am also deeply indebted to Frank Martin for his expertise in helping me write this book. Frank was great to work with and went beyond the call of duty. He was able to capture my voice with written words in an amazing manner. He also seasoned this work with his own words of wisdom and experience.

Joel Kneedler of Alive Communications has been a good friend and excellent liaison in representing me and introducing me to my publisher, Baker Books. I am so thankful for Joel and the great people at Alive Communications for the important work they do.

I also couldn't be happier with Baker Books. Jon Wilcox and the entire team at Baker have been consummately professional and great to work with in every manner. They have added an extra layer of input and expertise to this work that has enriched it in every way.

Last but not least, I want to thank our team at MarriageToday for their hard work and excellence. My son, Brenton, who is president of MarriageToday, is a joy for me to work with and is amazing in his role as my dear friend and associate. Brenton is an important part of everything I do. My assistant, Shelly Millheim, and our marketing director, Jana Schiewe, are two of the hardest workers in the world and have been invaluable in helping me with this book.

1

Great Marriages Don't Just Happen

> One of the ironies of contemporary family life is that many people who are good at intentional parenting are lousy at intentional marriage.
>
> William J. Doherty

> Marriage is the privilege and the honor of living as close to the heart as two people can get.
>
> John Eldredge

Imagine that you're sitting in the front row of a grand concert hall as one of the world's greatest violinists takes the stage. The crowd rises in applause as he slowly makes his way to the center platform. He adjusts the music stand, waits for the applause to die down, then lifts his bow to begin his first piece.

You find yourself mesmerized as he moves from one movement to the next with breathtaking skill and artistry. The music fills the hall, rising and falling with ease as his fingers glide effortlessly across the strings.

For two hours he plays with flawless rhythm and tone, never once missing a beat or note. His last piece comes to a close, and the crowd explodes with one last standing ovation as he exits the stage to his right.

Now imagine that as you're making your way down the aisle to leave, a pleasant man in an usher's uniform intercepts you at the end of your row and asks if you'd like to meet the great violinist. "I was watching you from a distance," he explains, "and I saw how moved you were by the music. I happen to have an extra backstage pass, so I thought I would offer it to you."

You eagerly accept and follow him as he ushers you through the crowd toward the front stage door leading behind the great curtain. You walk down a long hall and through several more doors, and soon you're standing outside the great violinist's dressing room. The usher knocks, the door opens, and suddenly you find yourself standing face-to-face with one of the world's most talented musicians. He shakes your hand, asking if you enjoyed the concert.

"Yes, I enjoyed it immensely," you answer. "In fact, I think that was the most beautiful music I've ever heard."

He nods and thanks you for your kind words. Then you say, "You're so lucky to be able to play with such perfection. It must be great to have been born with such talent, and then to have found a violin that fits your hands so perfectly. I wish I could find an instrument like that."

His smile fades, and his head cocks to one side as you continue.

"You know, I've always wanted to play music, and I plan to take it up someday. I think I could do it because I'm pretty talented. I just haven't been able to find the right instrument. Someday I hope to find the perfect violin, or maybe a cello, or even a trumpet—something that suits me perfectly. Then I'll be able to play as well as you do. I can't wait. . . ."

Is that what you would say? Is that what any of us would say?

Of course not. You wouldn't say that because it would be a monumental insult. You and I both know that violinists don't become great by accident. Greatness is not simply the result of a person stumbling upon the "perfect instrument" or being born with the right talent. It's the result of hours and hours of hard work and diligence.

Becoming a world-class musician takes years of dedication, persistence, and sacrifice. It takes untold hours of patience and practice.

It takes an intentional decision of the will to do whatever is needed to become the best musician possible.

When we see a great violinist playing a flawless sonata at Carnegie Hall, we all know instinctively that he's earned the right to be there because he's done the hard work it takes to be called great. To say otherwise is an enormous insult to his success.

The "Soul Mate" Myth

So what about great marriages? Does that same dynamic hold true?

Instead of standing before an accomplished violinist, what if you were attending the fiftieth wedding anniversary of a happily married couple? Two people who had successfully navigated decades of life together, years of stress and strife and worry, a half century of bills and work and raising kids, yet after all that time seemed more in love than ever. You see the glint in their eyes as they smile in each other's direction. Just like two schoolkids in love. What would you say was the secret to their success?

Amazingly, many of us might think, *How lucky they are to have found each other. How wonderful it must be to find your soul mate at a young age and then spend your life growing old together. I wish I could find my perfect mate. Then maybe I could have the happiness they've found.*

When you see two people who are still deeply in love after fifty years of marriage, it's tempting to think they were just lucky, but that's as naïve as it is insulting. Great marriages don't just happen any more than accomplished musicians become that way by accident.

Like any great skill, loving takes time and patience and diligence to thrive and grow. Both partners must make an intentional effort to create a meaningful, lifelong love affair. A great marriage is not the result of two "soul mates" who happen to find each other. It is built through years of consistency and devotion—through a lifetime of dedication, effort, and sacrifice. Through a conscious decision to do whatever it takes to make the marriage the best it can possibly be.

This book is for those who desire to do just that—to make their marriage the best it can possibly be. It's for those who don't want to settle for second best. It's for those who have made a conscious decision to develop a deep and meaningful love affair with their spouse and are willing to do the hard work it takes to get where they want to be.

The Confluence of Two Souls

In the mountains of Colorado, two mighty rivers run through a large portion of the state—the Roaring Fork and the Frying Pan. They are powerful and independent rivers, and they come together just outside of Basalt, Colorado, in the Roaring Fork Valley.

You can stand on the bank and see the fork at which these two massive bodies of water crash into each other and become one mighty river. Thrill-seeking rafters come from all over the state to ride these rapids.

As you stand at the confluence of these two rivers, you're struck by the sheer violence and power of these two waterways viciously colliding as they attempt to flow together and become one giant river. It's an awesome sight to behold.

And it's a perfect picture of the dynamics at work when two autonomous souls get married.

In marriage, you often have two independent and strong-willed people coming together at a confluence and attempting to become one flesh. They are two forceful spirits—each with their own dreams and identities, each with their own thoughts and ideas about the future, each with their own needs and weaknesses—and they stand at the altar declaring their desire to become one.

If that isn't a formula for conflict, I don't know what is.

That's why it takes work to grow a great marriage. That's why any marriage that lasts longer than a Tootsie Roll is bound to have struggles. People are inherently different, and when two different people come together into one life, there is going to be trouble.

The good news is, the longer these two "rivers" run together, the quieter the waters become. If they can just hang on and make it downstream, the rapids become easier to navigate. And the better they become at navigating those rapids.

The problem in most troubled marriages is that couples get stuck in the currents. They get caught up in the rapids and don't know how to move forward. They get stuck on a large rock or boulder and can't seem to force their way free.

One has a dream or desire that they refuse to turn loose, and they cling tightly to it, afraid that if they let go they'll lose their identity. The other has dreams of their own, and they too hang on for dear life. The two refuse to work together and find safety downstream, and instead they find themselves in a constant battle to hang on to their independence, each desperately afraid of being swallowed up by the other.

This is where most divorces occur. It's to this point that almost every broken marriage can be traced. People get stuck in the middle of a violent rapid and refuse to let go.

What they don't understand is that the only hope they have is to turn loose and trust the other as they learn to work together, allowing God to mold and shape them into a strong and dynamic couple.

A Magnificent Journey

I have an optimistic view of marriage. I don't believe marriage was intended to be chronically frustrating and difficult. I don't think it's something we're supposed to "endure" in order to become better people. And it certainly wasn't intended to be dull and ordinary.

I believe marriage was created by God to be enormously fulfilling and exciting. It's intended to be filled with fun and adventure and gratification. When done right, marriage is the most rewarding experience a person can have this side of eternity.

When two rivers come together and successfully blend into one, they create a river that is far more powerful and magnificent than either of them could have been on their own. Because I believe that, I'm in the business of helping people create great marriages. My wife, Karen, and I have dedicated our lives and our ministry to bringing a message of hope and encouragement to those who are struggling in their relationships. Years ago God brought our marriage back from the brink of divorce, and in the process he imparted to us a vision and desire to help others do the same.

An Indestructible Marriage

After more than thirty years of counseling, I've found that the one truth I hold most dear is that no marriage is beyond help. Today I am convinced that any marriage can have a 100 percent chance of success. I believe that any couple, regardless of the baggage they bring to the table, can rebuild a strained and broken marriage into a love affair that is stronger and more passionate than the days of their honeymoon.

I'm absolutely certain that any couple can have a marriage that is divorce-proof, affair-proof, boredom-proof, disappointment-proof, even Satan-proof. A love affair that is completely and certifiably indestructible!

I believe these things because I've seen them happen time and again, not just in my own life but in the lives of countless couples who made the decision to put a few timeless principles to work. Principles that are readily found within the pages of Scripture. Eternal truths that were given to us by God to supernaturally bind our hearts together.

These principles, once unwrapped and put into practice, unfold for us the mystery of a lifelong love affair.

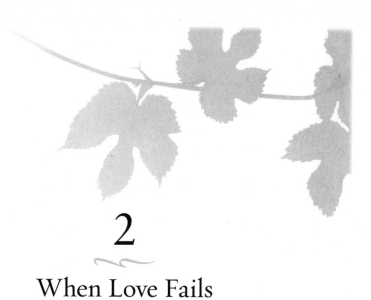

2

When Love Fails

Those who marry will face many troubles in this life.

1 Corinthians 7:28

Five out of ten marriages today are ending in divorce because love alone is not enough.

Emerson Eggerichs

It happened on an average Friday evening, right after dinner. The table had been cleared, the leftover food had been put away, and Lisa was busy loading the last few dishes into the dishwasher. One child was away at college, one was visiting a friend out of town, and the youngest two were sleeping over with friends. Lisa and her husband, Walter, were home alone for the evening.

Lisa turned to see Walter standing in the doorway of the kitchen. He looked somber and troubled, so she wiped her hands on a dish towel and turned to face him.

"We need to talk," he said.

"Okay," Lisa responded.

"You need to know that I'm in love with another woman," he began. "I've been seeing her since last year, and I can't keep it from you any longer. I've realized that I don't love you anymore. In fact, I don't think I ever did love you. Now I'm through pretending. I'm leaving you, Lisa. I don't want to discuss it, because I've made up my mind. I'm leaving tonight, and I want a divorce."

Lisa froze. For a solid five seconds—five seconds that felt like an eternity—neither said a word. She glanced at the ground, trying hard to keep her composure, then again fixed her gaze upward.

"You're kidding, right?"

"You know I would never joke about this," he answered. "I've never been happy in this marriage, and I want out. My bags are already in the car, and I plan to file for a divorce as soon as I can. I still love our kids, so I hope you won't make this hard on everyone."

Lisa couldn't believe what she was hearing. She knew things had been a bit distant between them lately, but she had no idea he felt this way. And she never imagined he'd been having an affair.

"So you're in love with another woman?" she asked, her voice quivering. "Is that why you want to leave?"

"Yes, I'm in love with someone else. But that's not why I'm leaving. I'm leaving because I don't love you. I don't think I ever have."

For the next twenty minutes, Lisa listened silently as Walter continued to wound her with his words. He explained how he had never been satisfied with their sex life, how he had felt trapped in a loveless marriage, how he had spent years pretending to be happy but just couldn't pretend anymore, how he needed someone more affectionate, more vivacious, more exciting. How he was certain that God wanted him to be happy.

That night Walter left, and he hasn't been back since. The two are now negotiating details of their divorce through lawyers. Lisa is alone, living in a small apartment with her two youngest kids and going to night school to learn a trade to support herself. Walter is looking for contentment in the arms of a woman fifteen years his junior, a woman who hasn't yet discovered his many flaws, a woman who is still ten years away from having to cover the gray streaks in her hair. A woman he's certain can bring him the happiness he deserves.

Broken Promises

Walter and Lisa's story is sad but not uncommon. In fact, it's a story that's growing more familiar by the day. Each month we receive many letters at our MarriageToday ministry headquarters from people just like Walter and Lisa. Couples on the brink of divorce. Couples who are struggling in their relationship, trying desperately to undo the damage that's been done. People who have been wounded by infidelity, pornography, abuse, or one of the many other marriage killers in today's society.

A lot of recent studies seem to suggest that the divorce rate in America has started to decline over the last few years, but that's only because fewer people are getting married. Many young people are choosing to cohabitate instead of getting married, and a large percentage of people simply choose to stay single. Today's married couples are under more stress and face more temptation than at any time in recent history, and largely because of this, people are simply afraid of making the commitment.

But perhaps the most disturbing statistic on marriage is the large number of empty nesters who are choosing to divorce. A recent study conducted by the National Center for Family and Demographic Research at Bowling Green University showed that the divorce rate for those over fifty has doubled in the last two decades. Today, 25 percent of all divorces are between couples over the age of fifty.[1]

In the past, marriages that lasted that long almost always went the distance, but that's not the case anymore. Empty nesters are divorcing at their highest rate ever.

I recently counseled a couple who filed for divorce just a few months after sending their youngest child off to college. As their pastor, I had asked to speak with them in hopes of saving their marriage. When I talked to them about it, they seemed completely ambivalent about the breakup. They calmly explained to me that they knew this day would come, that they had long since fallen out of love, and that they had stayed together only for the sake

1. Susan L. Bowen, "Divorce in Middle and Later Life: New Estimates from the 2009 American Community Survey," Center for Family and Demographic Research (Bowling Green, OH: Bowling Green State University).

of the kids. Now that their child-rearing days were over, they saw no more reason to remain married. Nothing I said could convince them otherwise.

Like Walter and Lisa, almost all couples go into marriage pledging to stay together through thick and thin. Yet fewer and fewer couples seem willing to honor that promise.

Where Did We Go Wrong?

So what happened with Walter and Lisa? That's a question that begs an answer.

What would cause a man to so easily turn his back on his family? Why would a man who had so much going for him, a man who had invested twenty-five years of his life in a relationship, simply decide one day to leave and start over? What would cause a once strong and thriving love affair to fade and die so easily?

The truth is that what happened with Walter and Lisa is not only common, it's predictable. In fact, it's the natural result of a love relationship left unchecked and unguarded. It's what can—and will—happen to any love affair over time without regular and decisive care and maintenance.

I often compare love to a garden. When tended properly, a garden gets richer and fuller with each passing year. With each season it bears more fruit, fuller branches, deeper roots, thicker vines, and more beautiful plants and flowers. There is nothing more spectacular than a lush, green, flourishing garden that has been tended well and carefully tilled by a skilled gardener.

But what happens when the gardener stops working? When the garden goes untended? Even the lushest and most thriving garden will quickly begin to atrophy and wilt. Eventually it will die altogether.

Love doesn't have to be that way. It was never intended to last only for a season or to grow stale with age. Love was designed to grow deeper and stronger with time. To become even more intimate and rewarding. To meet many of our deepest needs and desires. To not only last but to grow healthier and fuller with age.

The question is, how exactly do we do that?

Irreconcilable Differences

When I was nineteen years old, I worked in a hardware store. One day I was going through the order sheets and saw an order for something called a "male fitting." I didn't know what that was, so I asked my boss about it. He grinned and took me into the back room. He pulled out a male fitting and showed it to me. Then he pulled out another type of fitting and said, "This is a female fitting." He put the two together to show me why they were called that.

I was completely stunned. And I'm pretty sure I turned beet-red.

From that day on I was absolutely convinced that all plumbers were perverts. And every time someone came in asking for a male or female fitting, I had to bite my tongue to keep from laughing.

Even hardware store guys understand that men and women are inherently different. Not only do they look different, but they have distinct purposes. And they are created to fit together. They are intended to work as a team.

When couples understand this truth and learn to embrace their differences, they're able to create something dynamic and beautiful together—something that neither of them could have made on their own. They find a renewed synergy and purpose within the relationship.

A man can accomplish great things on his own, but when he binds himself to a godly wife, the possibilities become even greater. A woman can have a perfectly happy and productive life on her own, but if she can build a meaningful life with a husband, a brand-new world of opportunities is opened up to her.

When we embrace our differences, we become stronger as a team. It's when we reject and criticize those differences that trouble comes.

When couples file for divorce, the most common reason they state on the divorce petition is "irreconcilable differences." When forced to disclose what happened to tear them apart, they have to admit that they were simply unable to reconcile the differences between them. So they've given up and decided to go their separate ways.

Most of these couples married because they found their differences exciting. They were drawn to each other because of their different natures, the unique ways they looked and thought and acted, and their distinct spirits, characters, and personalities. It was their differences that made them want to build a life together.

But they soon realized how difficult it is to blend two unique individuals into one union. It's not easy to take two raging rivers and flow them into one independent body of water. So they gave up trying.

Marriage is about learning to reconcile the differences that make us so special and unique. It's about learning not only to accept those differences but to welcome them, grow through them, and embrace the new and exciting possibilities our differing personalities can bring.

Finding Hope in the Chaos

Let me venture a guess. You didn't pick up this book because you have nothing else to do. I doubt that you have so much free time on your hands that you're just looking for extra ways to fill it.

If you're reading this book, you probably have a good reason for it. Maybe you picked it up at one of my marriage seminars or ordered it from our *Marriage Today* television program. Perhaps your pastor or marriage counselor suggested it. Or maybe you simply stumbled across it in your local bookstore and found the title intriguing. However you came across it, I seriously doubt that you're reading it for pleasure.

If you've found yourself on this page, I'm going to assume that at least some of you are struggling through some difficult issues in your marriage. Maybe you've found yourself frustrated or indifferent or worse. You could be in the middle of a relationship so fractured and damaged that you doubt any amount of work can save it. Perhaps you're in the throes of divorce.

Whatever it is that brought you here, let me give you a word of encouragement from someone who understands exactly what you're going through. No matter how bad things seem at the moment, there is hope. No matter how frustrated you feel, no matter how much pain and heartache you've experienced, no matter how strained your relationship has become, you can make it through. More than that, you can rebuild your broken love affair and come out on the other end stronger and happier than you ever imagined possible.

I know what it's like to feel utterly hopeless and broken, to be so disenchanted with your relationship that you think divorce is the only option. I understand the frustration of feeling completely out of sync with your spouse and the sting of hurtful and biting words being slung back and forth across the room—words you wish you could take back the second they leave your lips. Trust me, I understand your pain.

Karen and I have been married for over thirty-nine years, and I can honestly say without hesitation that we are happier and closer today than we ever imagined possible. But it hasn't always been that way. Early in our marriage we made mistakes that bordered on irreparable. Mistakes that very nearly shattered the foundation of our marriage.

By the grace of God, we made it through those stormy times and found the strength to move forward. And in the process, we learned some profound, life-altering truths about ourselves and God's purpose for our marriage. Truths that are surprisingly simple yet revolutionary enough to radically alter the direction of any marriage.

Stay with me while we explore these concepts together. I promise it will be worth your while, no matter where you are in your relationship.

3

A Journey of Surrender

He who trusts in his own heart is a fool.
Proverbs 28:26 NKJV

He who trusts in the LORD will be exalted.
Proverbs 29:25 NASB

In my years of counseling married couples and teaching on marriage issues, I've discovered two common denominators in every marriage relationship—two desires that are universally held by every couple.

The first is that every couple starts out marriage determined to succeed. No one stands before the altar planning to fail. Some may show up at the church with a case of cold feet, but they can't imagine themselves ever divorcing. Those who do usually back out long before the wedding day. But in my experience, every couple who makes the matrimonial pledge is fully committed to staying married for the long haul. That's why marriage vows are filled with idealistic language and promises of a lifelong commitment. And I'm convinced that almost every person who recites those vows is sincere to the core of their being.

The second universal truth I've discovered is that every couple wants to have a great marriage. No one sets out to have an okay marriage or even a good one. They long to have an exceptional marriage, a lifelong, passionate, insanely rewarding love affair with their spouse. They want a marriage better than those of their parents and peers, even better than their fantasies. And they're usually convinced that the person standing next to them is the one person on earth who can fulfill that desire.

Youthful Bliss

Karen and I were both nineteen years old when we got married. Just a couple of kids in love. We had almost nothing going for us. I was flat broke—an underachieving college kid working at the Scrub-A-Dub Car Wash for minimum wage, which was about $1.60 an hour. I drove a beat-up 1964 Dynamic Eighty-Eight Oldsmobile that my mother gave me—right after she nearly totaled it. The passenger door was completely crushed, and Karen had to crawl past the steering wheel to get in. Karen had a job at the Bank of the Southwest making $225 a month. Our combined income wasn't even enough to put us in the category of "poverty-stricken"—we were closer to "destitute." But none of that mattered to us.

I had been a Christian for only one week on the day of our wedding, and I'm not sure anyone in the room thought Karen was making a good decision. Her parents didn't like me, her friends tried to talk her out of it, and half of those in attendance—at least the half on her side of the room—were fervently praying that she'd come to her senses and make a mad dash for the exit.

I may very well have been the least qualified groom ever to put on a suit, but that didn't shake my confidence one bit. I was completely certain that our marriage was destined to last. I was sure that Karen was the luckiest bride ever to float down the aisle and that I was the one person in the world who could make her happy. And Karen was thoroughly convinced that she was doing the right thing, no matter what her parents and friends thought.

Karen and I were completely certain that our marriage was destined for greatness—that we would never fight, never get tired of each other, never disagree about money or kids or any of the petty things other couples argued about. We were the perfect match, flawless in every way, and nothing could stand in our way. Confidence was all we had going for us, but we had it in abundance.

It took only about two weeks for us to realize just how misplaced that confidence was.

When Battle Lines Are Drawn

I don't remember the first argument Karen and I had after we were married, but I do remember wondering if it would ever stop. Once we started fighting, we just seemed to keep on fighting. One argument would simply flow into the next one, like a long and raging river that had no end. We fought about everything—money, friends, relatives, food, furniture, having no furniture, room temperature, even the weather. Our marriage turned into one long battle that neither one of us could seem to win. It was the most tedious, frustrating, and soul-numbing season of our lives. And we had no idea how to make it stop.

Obviously there were good times between all the fights, but they seemed few and far between. And they became even fewer with each passing month. Looking back, I can easily see that I was the primary problem. I was something of a brute and ridiculously selfish. I simply wanted my way, and when I didn't get it, I made sure Karen didn't get her way either. Quite honestly, I was verbally and emotionally abusive to her; I just didn't see it that way at the time. I thought she was the stubborn one, and I was convinced that I'd simply married the wrong person.

Somewhere around the third year of our marriage, we hit rock bottom. Emotionally we were both wrung out. We were just numb and out of love. Karen had nothing left to give and nothing left to say, so she usually just said nothing. I'd get angry about something and she'd simply roll her eyes and go into her own world. That fueled my anger even more. We knew our marriage was in serious trouble, and we often wondered why we bothered to stay together.

I remember sitting in a chair in our living room during this period, fuming about another petty argument we'd had. I found myself thinking about a girl I'd dated back when I was sixteen. She was the girl I broke up with when I first became smitten with Karen. I took this girl out only a few times, and we could never seem to get along, but now I started fantasizing about her. *Maybe I should have stayed with her. I wonder if she's the one I should have married. I wonder what she's doing today. . . .*

I think that's when I first realized just how far Karen and I had drifted apart. It was a sad day for me, and for the first time I started seriously thinking about packing my bags and leaving. And to make things even more painful, I was sure that Karen was having the same thoughts.

Point of No Return

Karen and I had countless arguments during this time, and they continued to grow more bitter and brutal by the day. But one particular argument stands out as the one that very nearly destroyed our marriage. It was the most frightening and sobering experience of my life.

I had gone golfing with friends after work, and Karen was home tending to our daughter, Julie. At the time, I was addicted to golf and was actually pretty good at it. But Karen wasn't impressed with my skills on the links. To her, golf was just a hobby that kept me away from home far too often. I played several times a week, usually after work, and almost every Saturday, which meant Karen and Julie spent many evenings at home alone. A lot of our arguments revolved around my golfing obsession, and I resented Karen deeply for not understanding my love for the game.

This particular day, I was out later than usual, and the later it got, the more frustrated she became. I had had a great game that evening and actually came home in a pretty good mood. Then Karen confronted me when I walked in the front door.

She told me how cold and uncaring it was for me to be gone so many hours when my family needed me at home. She told me how frustrating and demeaning it felt to be taken for granted, and she wondered why I married her in the first place if I never planned to be home. She didn't shout or scream, but she made it clear that she was tired of competing for my attention and sick of being left alone every evening while I hung out with friends.

I was completely blindsided by her accusations and immediately got angry. I began firing off accusations of my own, and within minutes we were in another long and vicious argument.

Soon my anger got the best of me, and I pointed toward our bedroom and shouted, "I'm finished! Just go pack your bags and leave! If you're not happy with me, then you can go back to your mother and father!"

Karen ran into our bedroom and slammed the door behind her. She threw herself across the bed, buried her face deep into a pillow, and started sobbing. I could hear her crying from the other room. I had heard her cry many times before, but never like this. Her sobs were deep and unending. I instinctively knew I had gone too far. I was certain our marriage had finally reached the point of no return.

As I sat in our living room listening to Karen's cries of pain, something started to stir deep in my spirit. I could hear her shuffling in the bedroom and knew that she was packing her bags to leave. The sound sent a chill down my spine. I knew that if I didn't do something fast, I would lose Karen forever.

Somehow I found the strength within me to walk into the room and ask Karen to stay. I told her I was sorry and apologized for the hateful things I had said. As the words left my mouth, I realized that it was the first time I had ever apologized to her.

Karen immediately softened, and the two of us embraced. She buried her face in my chest and cried for what seemed an eternity. We eventually went to bed, both of us emotionally exhausted from the most bitter and hurtful fight of our married life. Even though we had both apologized for the things we'd said, we knew we could never take them back. I lay in bed that night wondering if our relationship could ever really be repaired.

In my heart of hearts, I honestly didn't think there was any hope left for us. I didn't know how much longer we could last, and I was almost certain divorce was right around the corner.

Raising the White Flag

So what happened to turn things around in our marriage? How did we ever get from that point to where we are today—from two battle-weary soldiers in a war that wouldn't end to two giddy old married people who can hardly keep their hands off each other? What miraculous event brought us back together?

The truth is, it wasn't any one thing that made the difference, just a long series of small decisions and attitude changes, followed by more decisions and more attitude changes. It's a process that I'll discuss in detail in the chapters to come. But like all journeys, it began with one critical, monumentally important first step that can be summed up in one simple and succinct sentence.

We gave up.

At some point in time, we both realized that we simply could no longer make it on our own. We finally came to grips with the reality that we were completely incapable of putting our marriage back together again—at least in our own power—so we gave up trying. We put down our weapons and raised the white flag. We surrendered.

Our marriage had been so beaten and battered that we instinctively knew a decision would have to be made. There was no doubt that it was time to throw in the towel; we just had to decide which towel to toss. Would we throw in the towel of marriage and go our separate ways? Or would we throw in the towel of self?

Trust me, this was not an easy decision for either of us. When you've effectively convinced yourself that you've married the wrong person, it's a pretty small step from there to simply walking away and never looking back. Leaving would be the easiest and most personally gratifying choice. When you walk out, you can leave with your dignity intact. It's the ultimate act of getting even for all the hurt you've suffered.

Looking back, I'm surprised I didn't take that approach. I'm even more surprised that Karen didn't. No one could have blamed her for leaving an emotional bully like me.

But somehow, through some miraculous act of intervention that I still don't quite understand, we both found the strength to do the right thing. We surrendered our marriage to God. We each opened our hands and our hearts and gave ourselves over to his will. We recommitted ourselves to the relationship, and little by little, day by day, we started rebuilding the love that had died.

It wasn't a onetime decision, and it didn't happen overnight. It was a process of daily dying to self, of getting up each morning and deciding to be a little better and nicer to each other than we were the day before, of being just a little more forgiving, a little more loving, a little more selfless and caring.

In short, we did with our marriage what God asks each of us to do in our own Christian walk. We surrendered a little more of ourselves each day, and instead of focusing on our own selfish desires, we focused on the needs of the other. I started learning Karen's needs and looking for ways to fill them. And she did the same for me.

We gave up trying to make it on our own and instead leaned on God to change our marriage—to rebuild the love affair that we had so callously destroyed. And that has proven to be the most supernaturally rewarding decision we ever could have made.

The First Step toward Success

Surrender is a small word with enormous implications and even greater long-term consequences. It's not a word to be thrown around lightly.

When Karen and I finally raised the white flag of surrender, it was a monumental occasion, but only the first step toward putting our marriage back together. Lots of damage had already been done, and the wounds didn't heal quickly. We didn't change overnight. It's not easy to spend years of your life in a war of wills and then suddenly decide to stop fighting. It doesn't happen that way. Old habits die hard. It took a lot of hard work and discipline, many days and nights of retraining our thoughts and tongues, before we started to see a difference.

But the changes did come, and with them came a brand-new perspective. We started liking each other again, and the more we liked each other, the more we wanted to do for each other. We started enjoying each other's company again, and before long all the romantic feelings we'd once had started coming back. One day at a time, we rebuilt the love we had smothered.

When I counsel couples in conflict, often ones on the brink of divorce, I relate to their struggles far more than many of them understand. I usually tell them that Karen and I were once right where they are, though I'm not sure they always believe me. As I listen to tales of wounding words and unmet needs, stories of abuse, neglect, apathy, and selfishness, it brings back painful memories of my own sinful failings so many years ago.

Often it's all I can do to sit still and listen. The pastor in me knows that it's my job to let the couple vent, to simply allow them to express their feelings, and afterward to give them a few words of advice along with some assignments for them to complete before the next session. Counseling is a process, and it's crucial to help couples work through issues at a healthy pace. So that's what I do.

But let me be completely honest. The Texas boy in me has a hard time staying silent. So often I find myself wanting to grab them by the lapels and say, "Listen, this is not that hard! What you need to do is surrender! Stop trying to fix this on your own and give your marriage to God. That's the only way you're ever going to make it."

I want to do this, but I don't, because I know it won't work. Surrender is not something you can do for someone else. It has to be a personal decision of the will, a declaration cried out from the core of our being. Sadly, most people will refuse to come to that point until they've hit rock bottom. Surrender is usually the last resort of a dying relationship. But it shouldn't be.

Time to Give Up

Wherever you are in your marriage, let me encourage you to make a brash and bold determination. Decide today to give up. Stop trying to make things work in your own power.

Whether you've found yourself at the end of your rope, struggling through a marriage on the brink of divorce, or simply feeling distant from your spouse and wanting to rekindle a dwindling flame, the answer you're looking for is found in this one simple word.

Surrender.

Surrender your will, your desires, your need for approval, your battle for control, your bitter thoughts and attitudes, your worries for the future, your regrets from the past, your concerns about the present. Surrender your marriage. Then surrender yourself.

Begin your journey where all journeys toward supernatural blessing must begin. Give your marriage to God, and let him do with it what you could never hope to accomplish on your own.

4

The Power of Covenant

Eve was not taken out of Adam's head to top him, neither out of his feet to be trampled on by him, but out of his side to be equal with him, under his arm to be protected by him, and near his heart to be loved by him.

Matthew Henry

That is why a man leaves his father and mother and is united to his wife, and they become one flesh.

Genesis 2:24

I once agreed to be a guest on a secular television program, and just minutes before going on the air the producer said to me, "By the way, Pastor Evans, would you mind not mentioning God?" I wasn't sure I had heard her right, so I said, "Excuse me?"

"I understand that you're a pastor," she said, "but a lot of our viewers might be put off by religion, so we'd appreciate it if you didn't mention God."

I smiled and nodded, all the while thinking, *This lady obviously doesn't know me very well.*

I mentioned God in the very first sentence.

It's not that I was trying to be difficult (okay, maybe a little), but I have two deeply held convictions that wouldn't allow me to stay silent.

The first is that I never miss an opportunity to share my faith with others. Anytime I have a chance to relay the truths of God's Word to those who haven't heard or accepted them, I take advantage of the opportunity.

The second is that I never give advice on building a strong marriage without discussing the true source of that advice. I'm honestly not sure I know how to separate the two. Marriage was created by God, and if you want to know how marriage works, you have to begin by examining what God has to say on the subject. Any other approach is going to leave you empty and confused.

I'm something of a research junkie, so the shelves in my office are filled with books and articles on the topic of marriage. Much of it comes from secular counselors and writers. Some of the best research on marriage and divorce has been conducted by secular organizations, and I glean a lot from their polls and statistics. But quite honestly, much of the advice they give on the dynamics of marriage is pretty pathetic—and distressing. I try to be open-minded, but often I find myself thinking, *What a waste of good trees.*

It's not as if these writers are ill-intentioned or uneducated. It's just that they're starting at the wrong place, and they're almost always building on a weak foundation—if they have any foundation at all. Analyzing marriage apart from God is the equivalent of being blindfolded and spun around in a circle, then asked to hit a target with a bow and arrow. The chances of getting even a little close are pretty remote, and you're likely to do a lot of damage in the process.

That's why so much of the advice you read from secular writers and counselors is contradictory. Read five different books on how to resolve marital conflicts and you'll likely get five different answers—some of them in direct opposition to each other. No wonder so many married couples are frustrated and confused.

Still, the biggest problem I have with secular marriage counselors has nothing to do with the conflicting viewpoints they give but with the one view they all seem to have in common. Almost every secular teaching on marriage sees divorce as a viable option for couples who can't seem to make their marriages work. They do a noble job of encouraging couples to work through their differences and even outline some good principles of conflict resolution, but at the end of the day, if a couple just can't see eye to eye, they say, "Maybe you've simply married the wrong person."

On the surface, apart from God's wisdom, this kind of thinking makes perfect sense. But it's a direct affront to everything God teaches about the sanctity and covenant of marriage.

One Flesh

It's no accident that God chose to reveal his plan and purpose for marriage just a few paragraphs into the Old Testament. He didn't waste any time leading up to the subject. I'm convinced he did that because he didn't want any confusion or debate on the matter. Marriage was an integral part of his overall plan for creation. He didn't just create marriage; he wove it into the very fabric of our existence.

Most of us are familiar with the creation story. God created the world and everything in it. Then he created Adam and put him in the Garden of Eden—a place of unimaginable beauty and abundance. Adam was charged with naming the animals and was given everything he needed for a long and happy existence.

One day God looked around and saw that his creation was perfect and complete in every way. Every way but one. "The LORD God said, 'It is not good for the man to be alone. I will make a helper suitable for him'" (Gen. 2:18). So God put Adam to sleep and removed a rib from his body. He used this rib to form Eve.

And why did he do that? God formed every other living creature from dust, including Adam, so why not create Eve that way as well? What was so special about this final creation?

God did what he did because Eve was not just another creation— she was the completion of a creation already in progress. Man was created whole but not *complete*. So God completed him. "The man said, 'This is now bone of my bones and flesh of my flesh; she shall be called "woman," for she was taken out of man'" (Gen. 2:23).

41

When God created Adam and Eve, he created them as two uniquely different creations but forever bound by a common identity—a kind of oneness that is distinct and exclusive, unlike anything else in all of creation. Adam and Eve were two separate individuals, unique in every way, with different needs, appearances, and personalities, yet God stood them side by side and declared them one flesh: "That is why a man leaves his father and mother and is united to his wife, and they become one flesh" (Gen. 2:24).

In the Garden of Eden, God performed the world's first marriage ceremony. It was God himself, the Creator of the world and everything in it, the "Father of the bride," who presided over the service. And in doing so—in speaking this supernatural blessing over Adam and Eve—he spoke into existence his ultimate design for marriage as a covenantal relationship.

Cutting Covenant

Covenant is not a word to be taken lightly. In the Old Testament, the Hebrew word for *covenant* means "to cut." When two parties entered into a solemn and binding agreement, they would literally "cut covenant." It was a ritual in which covenantal partners would hew an animal in two and place the severed halves on each side of a pathway. Then both partners would walk together between the bloody halves of the carcass. The pledge they were making was a solemn and binding one, and it involved a twofold promise. First, they promised to walk faithfully together within the boundaries of the oath. Second, they pledged to suffer the same fate as the animal if they broke the covenant.

When God made his covenant with Abram, this was the ritual he used to seal his promise. The covenant involved blood and sacrifice and a solemn pledge. God promised to form a mighty nation from Abram's descendants and to make Abram the father of a nation that would bless all nations of the world. In entering into the covenant, God was promising to suffer the same fate as the animals if he broke that promise.

Covenant is the tool that God uses to establish a relationship with his people. In the Bible, every relationship that God entered into was established on the basis of covenant. Why? Because covenant creates a bond that is far more intimate and binding than a simple promise.

When God put Adam to sleep to remove his rib, he literally cut open his side and then closed up the wound with flesh. It was a surgery that involved real blood and pain and sacrifice. God was setting the stage for a blood covenant. Then after using Adam's rib to form Eve, God "brought her to the man" (Gen. 2:22) to unite them.

God saw that Adam needed a partner, so he created one especially for him. Eve was formed with Adam in mind—a partner with all the features and attributes he needed to complete the tasks God had charged him with. Eve was Adam's perfect mate. She was exactly what he needed to live a happy, productive life physically, emotionally, and spiritually.

Then God bound Adam and Eve together in a sacred and covenantal ceremony of marriage.

Just Two Kids in Love?

When Karen and I stood side by side in front of the preacher those many years ago, promising to love, honor, and stay together "until death do us part," I honestly had no idea what I was getting into. I remember thinking that I was making some pretty hefty promises, but I had made promises before. I'd also broken promises before, and the world never seemed to come to an end because of it. In hindsight, the vows I was making were little more than words I had to say if I wanted to get married. I was just repeating what the preacher told me to say so we could hurry up and get to the fun part—the kiss. Not to mention the honeymoon!

It's not that I intended to take my vows lightly. I understood that marriage was a sacred thing, and I fully intended to keep my part of the bargain. When I looked at Karen, I was smitten to the core, and I couldn't imagine ever falling out of love, so promising to stay with her seemed like a pretty easy hurdle. But the concept of God supernaturally binding our hearts and souls together in covenant was completely foreign to me.

Karen had a much keener appreciation for the vows we were making, but even so, neither of us fully understood the weight of the ceremony or what it meant to become one flesh in the eyes of God.

It also never occurred to me at the time that God was the one who had brought us together. When I first laid eyes on Karen, I thought she was the most beautiful woman I'd ever seen. She was perfect in every way. Physically, she was the girl I had always dreamed of marrying. The attraction was instant and unequivocal.

I'm still not sure what Karen saw in me, but somehow I was able to get on her radar screen, and she fell for me just as hard. The chemistry between us may have been shallow and immature, but it was enough to keep us completely hooked. So I bought a ring, she bought a dress, and we decided to make it official.

In our minds, nothing about our story was unusual or unique. We were just a couple of young kids who fell in love and decided to get married. A lot of our friends were doing the same thing, because that's what people do. You get to the right age, find the person of your dreams, and get hitched. It's just that simple.

But now I know that God doesn't see it that way. In the eyes of God, our story was far more significant and supernatural. And the ceremony was about far more than just two love-struck kids making promises that neither of them was equipped to keep.

A Marriage Made in Heaven

Not many of us take time to see our mate as one whom God created and formed specifically with us in mind. It's hard for us to imagine God being that intimately involved in our lives. But Scripture teaches us that he is. You can't come away from the story of Adam and Eve without a renewed perspective on this truth.

God formed Eve for a specific purpose, but more than that, he formed her with a specific mate in mind. She was created for Adam. When Adam saw her for the first time, I'll bet his heart skipped a beat and his palms started to sweat. He probably slurred his words and said something stupid. And she likely had the same response when she first saw him.

Adam and Eve were created to build a lifelong love affair with each other. To walk hand in hand in the garden, to laugh at each other's jokes, to keep each other warm at night, to work out problems when they disagreed, to sit together and count the stars on a moonlit night. They were created to grow in love and learn how to navigate life together as a married couple.

God brought Karen into my life for that same purpose. She was created specifically with me in mind. I was created specifically for her. God envisioned us as a couple long before we ever met.

I imagine that one day God looked down and saw that I was lonely and alone, and he said to himself, *It's not good for Jimmy to be alone. I think it's time I introduced him to Karen.*

Actually, he probably said, *That boy Jimmy needs some serious help. I'd better get Karen over there quick!* But the idea is the same. God not only knew exactly what I needed in a life partner, he knew when I needed it. Karen was created with all the gifts, talents, and attributes I most needed in a wife. And I was created with her needs in mind as well. Just as God had a specific vision and purpose for Adam and Eve, he had a special plan and purpose for Karen and me. He had some tasks he needed us to accomplish during our days on earth, some children he needed us to make, some goals he needed us to work toward. And these were goals that neither of us was equipped to accomplish on our own. We needed each other.

God brought us together and nudged our relationship along until he finally got us before him at the altar. And there he supernaturally bound our hearts and lives together in the sacred covenant of marriage.

If I had seen Karen in that light when we first met, I never would have treated her with such disrespect during the early years of our marriage. I never would have taken her for granted. I would have loved her more, treated her better, and been more patient, thoughtful, and tender. I would have listened when she had something to say and worked harder at meeting her needs. I would have cherished her, nurtured her, encouraged her, treasured her, and helped her become all that God intended her to be.

If I could have seen our relationship from God's perspective—the way God wanted me to see it—the difference would have been staggering. I would have dedicated my life to becoming the husband she most needs me to be.

The Larger Story

In our ministry to married couples, there's one truth that Karen and I are committed to helping couples understand. Something she and I learned firsthand.

We tell couples that it is never too late to start over. It's never too late to make your marriage work.

No matter how beaten and battered your marriage has become, no matter how distant and disenfranchised you feel, no matter how much pain you've felt or afflicted, you can decide today to change course.

The same God who supernaturally bound you together in the covenant of marriage is longing to help you turn your marriage into the glorious love affair it was always intended to become. And rebuilding begins by embracing one important truth.

Your marriage is not an accident.

It was God who brought you together. It was God who ushered you to the front of the church that day in front of all those witnesses. It was God who bound you together in the covenant of marriage.

And it was all planned long before you were even a sparkle in your daddy's eye. Your marriage was planned and purposed long before you were born. Any damage that has been done is a direct result of Satan's desire to destroy everything God creates.

You are living in a story that is much greater and larger than you could possibly imagine. God has a magnificent dream for your marriage. That dream is far more glorious than any dream you could plan or envision on your own. God has things he wants to do in and through your relationship. Things that are eternal and lasting and supernatural. Plans that are greater than any of us could hope to comprehend. If your marriage is struggling, it's only because you've lost sight of that reality.

Every time I see a marriage in trouble, I see two people who are completely caught up in the small story of their own lives. They are so focused on their own pain, their own needs, their own selfish desires, that it's impossible for them to see God's bigger picture. And the problem with living in the smaller story is that those people find themselves engrossed in petty and mundane things, like bills and cars and houses, and pouting when they don't get their way.

And no couple will ever find true happiness and fulfillment in the smaller story.

God doesn't live there. God exists only in the larger story, and that's where he desires to take you.

In the larger story, you are married to the one person God created just for you. In the larger story, it was God who brought you to the altar and molded your hearts and lives together into one flesh. In the larger story, God has a glorious plan and purpose for your marriage.

The larger story is about *you and your spouse and God*.

Only in the larger story can God bring your relationship to its full potential.

5

God's Dream for Your Marriage

I f you asked ten different people why God created marriage, you'd probably get ten different answers. And, assuming they were all believers, most would be partially right.

Some would say marriage is God's way of populating the earth. Others might say it was designed to keep people from getting lonely. Still others might talk about Mars and Venus and how our differing roles complement each other.

All these views are valid, but do they really explain God's ultimate purpose for marriage?

Populating the earth is easy. Just tell people to pair off and make babies. Animals do it all the time, even the ugly and disgusting ones, like scorpions and chickens. Heck, even plants do it.

Curing loneliness is even easier. All I need is a handful of golfing buddies and I'm set for life.

Mars and Venus are good visual aids when it comes to demonstrating our differences, but there's more to marriage than the pairing off of two unique beings.

If God's plan for marriage was simple, a simple solution would have worked. But it wasn't. God's vision and intent for marriage were far more complex and meaningful.

God's Purpose for Marriage

Genesis 1:27–28 says:

> So God created mankind in his own image, in the image of God he created them; male and female he created them. God blessed them and said to them, "Be fruitful and increase in number; fill the earth and subdue it. Rule over the fish in the sea and the birds in the sky and over every living creature that moves on the ground."

God blessed Adam and Eve with the gift of covenant relationship, and then he charged them with a divine task and purpose—to "fill the earth and subdue it." This was a task that neither could successfully complete on their own. They needed each other.

But this wasn't the only purpose God had in mind for them. God had a vision for Adam and Eve that far surpassed any earthly task he had given them. He had a purpose that transcended the natural realm and lifted them into the spiritual realm. A purpose that was so unique and significant and supernatural that you and I have no hope of ever truly grasping it on our own.

It was the apostle Paul who most eloquently and graphically explained this purpose. In his letter to the Ephesians, Paul addresses the topic of marriage, and in the process he gives the most revealing text in all of Scripture on how husbands and wives should treat each other. He writes:

Wives, submit yourselves to your own husbands as you do to the Lord. For the husband is the head of the wife as Christ is the head of the church, his body, of which he is the Savior. Now as the church submits to Christ, so also wives should submit to their husbands in everything.

Husbands, love your wives, just as Christ loved the church and gave himself up for her to make her holy, cleansing her by the washing with water through the word, and to present her to himself as a radiant church, without stain or wrinkle or any other blemish, but holy and blameless. In this same way, husbands ought to love their wives as their own bodies. He who loves his wife loves himself. After all, no one ever hated their own body, but they feed and care for their body, just as Christ does the church—for we are members of his body. "For this reason a man will leave his father and mother and be united to his wife, and the two will become one flesh." This is a profound mystery—but I am talking about Christ and the church. However, each one of you also must love his wife as he loves himself, and the wife must respect her husband.

5:22–33

I refer to this passage nearly every day in my ministry to couples because it perfectly outlines God's guidelines for a happy and fulfilling marriage. But the true power of the passage is found in the way Paul continues to compare marriage to our relationship with Christ. Over and over he makes the correlation. He encourages wives to submit to their husbands "as the church submits to Christ." He tells husbands to love their wives "as Christ loved the church." The analogies appear to be interchangeable.

Then he ends his discourse by repeating the words God spoke to Adam and Eve, so that you and I would see their true meaning.

"For this reason a man will leave his father and mother and be united to his wife, and the two will become one flesh." This is a profound mystery—but I am talking about Christ and the church.

verses 31–32

Do you see what Paul was trying to say? Do you get what he was trying to tell us about the *mystery* of marriage?

Marriage, above all else, is an archetype of Christ's commitment to the church. Our relationship with each other is intended to reflect our relationship with Christ. Through marriage we are given a small glimpse of God's eternal covenant with humankind.

Jesus sacrificed himself on the cross for our sins. His side was pierced and his blood was spilled so that you and I could have a relationship with him. In the same way, Adam's side was pierced and his blood spilled so that he could have a relationship with Eve.

Through the covenant of marriage, we find ourselves ushered into the secret places of God. In a very real and dynamic way, marriage allows us to supernaturally participate with God in his divine nature.

Marriage was created, above all other things, to demonstrate God's splendor and beauty. And it exists solely for God's glory.

Through marriage, God chose to put his covenantal promise on display for all the world to see. That is why marriage exists. That is why you are married.

God's Glorious Gift

Does that make you as nervous as it makes me?

If the concept of being seen as an earthly demonstration of God's love and commitment doesn't send chills down your spine, then you might want to take a humility pill, because it certainly isn't something I signed on for. Karen and I have worked hard at growing a strong marriage, but we certainly aren't perfect.

Thank goodness God never expects us to be. And he doesn't hold it against us when we fall short. If it weren't for God's grace and goodness, we'd all be left holding the bag for our sins.

What God desires is for us to start looking at our mates through new eyes. To start seeing them the way he sees them—as people created in his image. People created for a sacred and divine purpose. People created with all the gifts, talents, and attributes he intended them to have. People who are perfectly designed to meet our most basic earthly needs and desires. People who were molded and shaped specifically for us.

When we begin seeing our relationship as a glorious gift from God—the way he wants us to see it—an interesting dynamic happens.

We start treating our mates with more love and respect and compassion. We find ourselves becoming more patient and kind, more forgiving, more caring. We start looking for the good instead of constantly criticizing the bad. And our mates start doing the same thing.

We start remembering what it was that first brought us together, and those giddy feelings we felt the first time we met start to resurface. We find ourselves falling in love all over again.

And that's not all God does.

When we start seeing and treating each other the way God desires—when we begin to live out our marriage the way marriage was designed to be lived—God begins to use us in ways we never imagined possible. He takes our small, human efforts and turns them into supernatural blessings. Not only does he take our relationship to greater heights than we ever dreamed, but he begins to unfold his wider plan and vision for our marriage. We begin to see why he brought us together, where he wants to take us, and what he wants to accomplish through us.

God's Vision Revealed

Karen and I had been married only a week when God first revealed his vision for our marriage. But thanks to my hard heart and stubborn ways, it was years before we were able to embrace it.

Before I met Karen, I had never imagined that God had a plan for my life. Though I attended church most of my life, I didn't know much about Jesus and had never accepted him as my Savior. I would sit in church on Sunday, and the minute the service was over I'd be out the door and looking for trouble. All my friends were immoral, and I was the worst one in the pack. When I started dating Karen, I did all I could to hide this fact from her. Even when we got engaged, I was pretending to be something I wasn't, hoping she wouldn't catch on. I knew how to talk and sound like a believer, and I played the part well. But deep down she somehow knew I wasn't the man I pretended to be.

Then a week before our wedding, some friends threw me a bachelor party. Some of the stuff I did at that bachelor party was, in a word, immoral. I knew it was wrong, and the guilt weighed on my heart. It was the lowest moment of my young life, and I decided to confess to Karen what I had done.

She called off the wedding, and it shook me to the core of my being. Karen was the best thing that had ever happened to me, and the thought of losing her was more than I could bear. It was a profound wake-up call. For the first time in my life, I dropped to my knees and pleaded for God's forgiveness.

I was young, just nineteen years old, but my brokenness was real. I asked God to come into my heart, then pleaded with him to bring Karen back into my life. Karen must have seen my sincerity, because she forgave me and decided to go through with the wedding.

In hindsight, she should have placed the wedding on hold and put me on probation. A few months of premarital counseling would have saved us years of grief in our marriage. Thankfully, God somehow worked it all out in the end.

It was only a couple of weeks later, exactly one week after our wedding, that God supernaturally revealed his vision for our marriage. And it was unlike anything I'd ever experienced.

I was sitting in the backyard of our house with unkempt hair down to my shoulders and a pack of Marlboros in my pocket. My mind was completely in neutral at the time, not thinking of anything in particular. Suddenly I envisioned a huge sheet dropping down in front of my face, and on the sheet I saw myself standing in front of a multitude of people. Karen was by my side, and I was preaching. The vision was as real as anything I had ever experienced. I felt that I could have literally reached out and touched the sheet. The images were clear and unmistakable.

I went into the house and told Karen what I had seen. I was afraid she would think I was crazy and half expected her to laugh, but she didn't. She just listened and asked me what I thought it meant.

"I don't know," I said. "Do you think God is calling me to be a preacher?"

Even as the words left my mouth, I knew how absurd the idea sounded. But Karen didn't flinch a bit. "That's what it sounds like to me," she said. Then she suggested that we pray about it and see where God might take us.

I agreed, but in my heart I never really accepted the idea. I couldn't imagine myself as a preacher. I had always dreamed of making my fortune in business. Preaching was a noble profession, but it would never bring in the kind of money I intended to make. I had high hopes for a big house and lots of fancy cars, and you don't get those things on a preacher's salary.

I told Karen I would pray about it, so that's what I did—at least for a few days—but in my heart I was filled with doubt. I knew that God was working in my life, but it took me awhile to understand what he was doing.

Not to mention what he still planned to do.

God's Vision Embraced

It was years before Karen and I were finally able to embrace God's vision for us. In my stubbornness and immaturity, I spent the first part of our marriage completely caught up in my own selfish needs and desires. In fact, I was on the fast track to missing God's vision for us altogether. I was a horrible husband and a closet chauvinist, and I thought Karen was there just to meet my needs. I treated her with so much disrespect and so little love that I very nearly imploded our marriage.

I'm so thankful that God reached in and set us on the right course, eventually restoring our marriage. I am 100 percent certain that if he hadn't done that, I'd now be on my third or fourth marriage. And well on my way to destroying that one as well.

But God did intercede, and our marriage changed for the better. We started looking to God for guidance, and in the process we discovered his perfect plan for marriage. Because of it, God brought us closer together than either of us ever imagined possible.

And it was then that God started restoring his vision for us as a couple. Little by little he began bringing opportunities and people into our lives to nudge us in the right direction. Eventually I found myself preaching in a small church, even though the thought of preaching scared me to death. Then before I knew it, I was pastoring a church in Amarillo—a career that was so far from what I had ever envisioned for my life that I still have trouble remembering how it all happened.

Eventually God called Karen and me to start an outreach to married couples, so we stepped out in faith and founded MarriageToday

Ministries. Today we are living out the very vision that God gave me those many years ago while I was sitting in the backyard of our house.

Finding God's Vision

There's nothing on earth more exhilarating than discovering and embracing the purpose God has planned for your life. And there's no greater joy in marriage than living out God's vision for you as a couple.

But first you have to discover what that vision is.

God's plan for marriage is universal, and Paul outlines it in the fifth chapter of Ephesians. God has only one plan for marriage, and it's the same for every couple—to treat each other with love, respect, and dignity, and to make your marriage into an earthly archetype of God's covenant commitment to man.

But God's *vision* for each marriage is distinct and unique. The vision God has for your marriage is different from the vision he has for ours. It's one that only you and your mate can fulfill.

As a pastor, I've counseled countless married couples, and so often they ask me how they can discover God's vision for their marriage. Once couples start embracing God's perfect plan for their marriage, they long for him to take their relationship to the next level.

During my early years as a pastor, I honestly didn't know what to tell those couples. I'd encourage them to pray about it and would take time to pray along with them, but I didn't have much advice beyond that. It was several years later that God introduced me to a much better plan.

And he did it through a humble and unassuming fellow pastor named David.

6

Meeting God on the Mountain

Where there is no vision, the people perish.

Proverbs 29:18 KJV

Come, let us go up to the mountain of the LORD. . . .
He will teach us his ways.

Micah 4:2

David was the associate pastor of a large church in Edmond, Oklahoma, where I had spoken a few times. Clark, the senior pastor, was also a good friend. I was pastoring a church in Amarillo, Texas, at the time, and I often traveled to Edmond to speak and conduct marriage seminars.

Clark and David loved golf as much as I did, and Edmond has some of the best courses in the country, so we'd hit the links every time I was in town. My associate pastor at the time, Tom, who is still one of my best friends in the world, almost always traveled with me, so we had a perfect foursome whenever we wanted to play.

David was a great guy, and the two of us got along really well. But the thing I most admired about him was the way he talked about his wife, Linda. He constantly complimented her and went out of his way to build her up in front of others. Even on the golf course, where many men seldom talk about their wives, he'd look for ways to mention her, always with glowing remarks. He'd talk about how beautiful and caring she was, how much he liked her cooking, how good she was with the kids, how much he looked forward to going home to her in the evenings, how lucky he was to be her husband. No matter what topic we were discussing, it seemed he'd find a way to bring Linda's name into the conversation, always in a kind way. It was no different when the two of them were together. They complimented each other incessantly and never put each other down. It was obvious that they were crazy about each other.

Karen and I had a wonderful marriage at the time, but still I found myself jealous of their relationship. At one point I remember thinking, *David is the only guy I know who has a better marriage than I do*. I often wondered about his secret.

Then one day, after a game of golf, the two of us were riding in the backseat of the car when David mentioned in passing that he and Linda would soon be leaving for their vision retreat.

I asked him, "What's a vision retreat?"

He seemed surprised. "You've never heard of a vision retreat?"

"No, I haven't," I answered.

"You mean you're the 'marriage guy' and you've never heard of a vision retreat?" he said, half joking.

David explained to me that each year he and Linda would go away alone for several days to seek God's vision for them as a couple. They called it their "vision retreat," and it was a nonnegotiable component of their marriage.

During their vision retreat, they would seek God's guidance. They would pray together and talk through issues that needed to be discussed. They would use the time to make decisions about their family, marriage, careers, and anything else going on in their lives. He told me they had been doing this for years and that it had done more to strengthen their marriage than anything they had ever tried.

I was fascinated by the idea. As a pastor, I knew how important it was to have a vision for my church, and a lot of my time was spent praying and seeking God's guidance for our congregation. Our pastoral staff would meet regularly to discuss our church's vision, and we even had a detailed vision statement that we had crafted years earlier. We'd refer to it often and read it aloud in meetings to make sure we were staying on track. We wanted to make sure God was at the helm when it came to making decisions, so we spent many hours in prayer, seeking God's guidance and direction for our fellowship.

So why not implement that same principle in our marriage and family? The idea made perfect sense to me. Quite honestly, I was a little embarrassed that I hadn't thought of it earlier.

I couldn't wait to tell Karen about the idea, and immediately I began planning our own vision retreat.

Our First Retreat

That very weekend I made arrangements with friends to borrow their lake house just outside of Dallas so that Karen and I could get away for a few days. It was a beautiful and private location, with a great front porch and miles of trails where we could get away to walk and talk. It was the perfect place to be alone and seek God's guidance.

Karen and I had long since overcome the struggles of our early years and had a very strong marriage at the time, but there was still tension in a few areas. It was the mid-eighties, and we had young kids at home. My career as a pastor and speaker was demanding, keeping me away from home far more than either of us wanted. Money was also tight, which always leads to friction. So we had some issues we needed to work through, and we were committed to using this time productively.

That weekend away did more to strengthen our marriage than anything we had ever done, just as it had for David and Linda. It was only four short days, but at the end of that time we felt closer than we had in years. Not only that, but we had a clear direction for our marriage and family—a written set of goals and promises that we were committed to carrying out.

Money and finances had always been a source of tension for us, and they were subjects that we usually avoided altogether. I've always been a spender and never worried much about budgeting or saving, while Karen is thrifty and cautious about spending money. In this area we've always been extreme opposites, and it created a lot of conflict through the years. We didn't fight about it very much—only because we didn't talk about it. But during our vision retreat, we spent time praying and discussing our finances and came away with a clear plan of action—a compromise that we both felt good about.

Suddenly money was no longer a topic we avoided. We had a written plan, and we both committed to sticking to it. Afterward, finances were no longer a point of tension. We simply stuck to the plan that God had given us and stopped worrying about it.

The same was true when it came to my career. When we committed it to prayer, it was obvious to both of us that I had been spending too much time at work and would probably face burnout soon, so we drafted a clear plan of action for my schedule. It took work on my part to stick to it, but I was committed to heeding God's voice and staying the course.

Raising kids always creates tension between couples, but during our weekend away, we were able to discuss some important decisions we needed to make regarding schools and discipline and family times. Once we sought God's vision for our family, it became clear what we needed to do in several areas that had been hanging over our heads, often causing frustration. Afterward, we never argued about it again. We simply stayed true to the vision God gave us and moved forward.

Since that time, vision retreats have become a regular, nonnegotiable part of our marriage. Every year we plan a few days away to seek God's guidance, and doing so is clearly one of the best decisions we've ever made. It has honestly made a dramatic difference in how we relate to each other as a couple and has proven to be one of the greatest strengths of our marriage.

We also began promoting the idea as an integral part of our ministry to married couples, and we even created a manual to help couples plan their own vision retreats. It's a simple booklet that we call *Mountaintop of Marriage*, and it's designed to walk couples through the idea step-by-step. For more information on how to plan a vision retreat, visit the MarriageToday website at www.marriage today.com/visionretreat.

We've helped thousands of couples plan and implement vision retreats in their own marriages, and the feedback we get is phenomenal.

It's one of the most effective tools we have for helping couples through conflict.

Healthy Communication

There's a reason I think vision retreats are so critical to a healthy marriage. Through the prophet Amos, God posed the question, "Can two walk together, except they be agreed?" (Amos 3:3 KJV). The answer is no. If you're not walking together, you're going separate ways. When that happens in marriage, you have a battle of wills and a struggle for dominance. For a marriage to be healthy, you have to be going the same direction.

It's impossible to have a strong and vibrant relationship with another person without good communication and consensus. That's why building a strong marriage begins by learning how to talk things through and then coming to a clear agreement on important matters. Good communication is a learned skill. It's not a natural thing for any of us. In fact, most of us have never learned how to communicate effectively.

I often say that there are three types of communication: *reactive*, *radioactive*, and *proactive*.

Most of us engage primarily in *reactive communication*. Someone does or says something that offends us, and we react to it. Often our reaction is hostile and negative. This was always a big problem in my life, especially in my younger years. I am analytical by nature and tend to think that most of my opinions are facts, so when someone says something I disagree with, I'm quick to react. This is what I did with Karen, and it created a lot of trouble early in our marriage. It's also what I see in almost every couple who comes to me for counseling. Almost all of their communication is reactive, and reactive communication is never healthy.

Radioactive communication is also unhealthy. This is when topics become such a source of conflict that you simply can't discuss them anymore. With Karen and me, money had become a radioactive topic, so we simply never brought it up. Every time I spent too much money, it would make her angry, but she was afraid to say anything. She'd react by trying to squirrel away money without telling me, and that would raise my dander. But I didn't talk about it either, because I knew it would only lead to an argument. The result was that we would both quietly fume with anger, which led to deeper feelings of resentment. Almost every couple I've counseled in the midst of conflict has areas of radioactive communication in their marriage.

The only healthy form of interaction is *proactive communication.* This is where you see a topic that needs to be discussed and tackle it head-on. You set a specific time and place to talk over an issue, then discuss it calmly and objectively, and always with a loving and patient attitude. You explain your position, listen to the other person as they explain theirs, and commit to finding a healthy compromise. Proactive communication is the only effective way to deal with conflict because it's focused on finding a solution, not simply snapping back or avoiding a sensitive issue.

A vision retreat is all about proactive communication. It's a specific, scheduled time for couples to calmly discuss their differences and come to a workable solution. It's an invaluable tool for overcoming conflict.

If vision retreats aren't a regular part of your marriage, then they should be. And if you have any areas of sensitive or recurring conflict, I suggest you plan one sooner rather than later. You'll likely wonder why you didn't think of it earlier.

For a vision retreat to work, you have to do it right. That means planning ahead and laying some important ground rules before you go.

Are You Ready?

Before planning your time away, make sure your marriage is in a state healthy enough to withstand the scrutiny. Spend time in prayer, asking God's guidance and wisdom, before launching out and booking a room. Ask your spouse to pray about it as well, and get their thoughts on the subject.

This is a critical first step, since not every couple is ready to handle such an intense time of struggle and communication. Many couples who come to me for counseling are so wounded and battered by years of conflict that they could never handle an isolated weekend together without a mediator. In their emotional state, a vision retreat would likely do more harm than good. It often takes months of counseling to help them work through their anger and resentment enough to where they can even have a normal conversation. The last thing they need during the height of crisis is to be thrown into a room together and told to "talk things through."

For a vision retreat to work, couples need to be able to open up to each other and to give and receive comments in a nonthreatening way. Unless it's done in the right spirit and attitude, a vision retreat can actually create even more division and turmoil. It's like throwing gasoline on an already raging bonfire.

But once couples have learned how to respond to each other in a healthy way and understand basic communication skills, a vision retreat is a great next step in their marriage. It's my job as a counselor to recognize when they've reached that point.

If you're not sure that your marriage is healthy enough for a vision retreat, chances are it isn't. If that's your situation, what you need most is a good marriage counselor, not another opportunity to fight. I'm convinced that no marriage is beyond help, so don't give up hope. But also don't try to go it alone. A good counselor can help save even the most disenfranchised relationship, so do whatever it takes to find one. If you can't convince your spouse to go with you, then start by going alone. Your marriage is worth the effort.

The Preparation Stage

Once you've felt God's blessing and release, it's time to prepare for your time away. Begin by praying for wisdom and clarity. Ask the Holy Spirit to prepare your heart for what's to come and to soften your spirit enough to receive supernatural guidance.

This is perhaps the most important part of the process, so don't rush it. Spend several weeks in prayer and study, and consider fasting for a few days if you can. It's critical that you go into this time with the right attitude and spirit. You need a humble heart and an open mind to hear God's voice, so turn off the noise of life and spend time listening.

During this time, ask God to reveal any areas of sin and disobedience in your life. Ask him to show you areas of your life and marriage that need to be strengthened or purged. Is there anything you're doing to cause your spouse pain or heartache? Have you been neglecting their needs? Do you even know their needs? In what ways have you been selfish or prideful? Have you been the kind of husband or wife that God has called you to be?

This is a time to focus on yourself and your own shortcomings. Don't ask God to reveal your spouse's sins, because that's not what this is about. A vision retreat is about finding and healing your own faults and failings, not convincing your spouse of theirs.

With a sincere and open heart, ask God to reveal those areas of your life and marriage that you need to change, and then trust that he'll do just that. God always responds when we come to him with a humble heart.

Why Do We Have to Leave?

People often ask if they actually need to leave home in order to have an effective vision retreat. I tell them, "Yes, you do."

Theoretically, I suppose you could find a way to block off a few days at home and do this, but I honestly don't think it would work as well. By definition, a retreat is a time away from the familiar and into a place of isolation and neutrality. Home is filled with inevitable distractions like kids and phones and the internet. People know where you are, so they drop by unannounced. When you take a walk, you bump into neighbors on the street. It's impossible to truly get away from it all unless you make the effort to *physically* get away. The place doesn't have to be expensive, just quiet and isolated. And romantic.

And no, you can't take the kids. This is where grandmas can come in really handy.

An Open Book

There are no hard-and-fast rules for having an effective vision retreat. What works for one couple may not work for another. But key elements need to be incorporated.

Karen and I always start our retreats with an extended time of prayer and confession. We pray individually, then we pray together, always asking God to lead and guide us as we seek his wisdom for our marriage and family. Then we share those things that God has been revealing about our own failings as a partner. We tell each other what God has been teaching us and ways he has been convicting our hearts.

One thing we never do is point fingers or direct blame toward each other. I confess my sins and shortcomings and ask for forgiveness, then Karen does the same. We never focus on each other's faults or transgressions; we allow the Holy Spirit to do that. We focus only on our own.

During our first vision retreat, this was the most challenging and painful part of the entire weekend. Confession should be a regular part of every marriage, but it's not because it's a difficult thing to do. Sharing your weaknesses feels dangerous and vulnerable, and you wonder how it will be received. It takes a lot of humility to give that much power to another person.

Since that time, however, our time of confession is something we actually look forward to. To be completely open and honest with each other about our weaknesses and struggles is an amazingly freeing experience. And it has bound our hearts together in a powerful way.

Karen and I have never felt closer than we do today. Neither of us has anything left to hide. No secrets. No hidden sins and temptations. No false pretensions. We stand before each other completely naked and unashamed, emotionally and spiritually. And our vision retreats have played a huge role in building that kind of openness and intimacy.

Every strong and healthy marriage is built on accountability. Becoming one flesh means giving each other complete access to the most secret and intimate corners of your heart. It means opening your soul and allowing the other to see inside. It's the most frightening and threatening feeling on earth. But it's the only way to build the kind of intimacy and love and accountability that God intended you to have.

The Big Questions

Another critical element to vision retreats is praying for a clear vision. That's actually the primary purpose behind the idea.

During our first retreat, Karen and I asked some pretty big questions we had never really addressed before. Things like, "Why did God put us together?" and "What higher purpose does he have for our marriage and our family?"

Most couples go through their lives never asking these kinds of questions, probably because deep down we really feel pretty alone and insignificant in the grand scheme of things. We can't imagine that God has some powerful goal or plan he wants to accomplish through us. But that's not true. That's just a lie from the enemy—something he's been whispering in our ears to keep us from embracing God's greater design.

God has a plan and purpose for everything he creates, and that's especially true for those he created in his own image.

You and your spouse were created with specific gifts and talents and then brought together by God to combine those talents toward a higher purpose. God has a very unique and special vision for your marriage, and if you haven't discovered it, he's waiting to reveal it to you.

This is your time to seek out that vision. Karen and I did, and God brought us a sense of clarity and direction that we'd never had before. We came away from our first retreat with an amazing sense of purpose and insight. We knew exactly what God wanted us to do, and we couldn't wait to get busy working toward that goal.

God loves answering big questions, and it's impossible to have any direction on the small questions of life unless you've first tackled the big ones. If you don't know why God brought you together or what he wants you to accomplish as a couple, how can you effectively make wise decisions on those everyday questions of life?

We all know the small questions. *Where should we send our kids to school? Where should we live? How should we spend our time and resources?* These are all questions of *priority*, and you can't know how to answer them unless you've first addressed the bigger questions of *purpose*.

Once you've answered the big questions in your marriage, the answers to the small ones seem to come into focus naturally.

The Power of Journaling

I also encourage couples to journal and to keep good notes of what they sense God is saying to them during their vision retreats.

Journaling is a good habit in life, but it's especially important during times of seeking and transition. The decisions you make during a vision retreat can be monumental, even life altering, and you need a good record just to help you stay on course. It also gives you concrete documentation of the decisions and promises you've made. Something you can refer to from time to time just to refresh your memory.

A journal also serves as a faith-building tool. Anyone who has kept a prayer journal knows how powerful it can be to go over the prayers you lifted up five, ten, and twenty years ago and see how God has faithfully answered them. The same is true when you journal about your vision retreats. You can go back through the years and see how God has moved in your life and marriage, and the different decisions he has guided you through. It's a powerful tool for seeing his direct involvement in your family and relationship. Seeing what God has done in the past gives us faith that he'll continue to guide and direct us in the future.

As the seasons of life change, so do those things that concern us. The things Karen and I pray about today are much different than they were twenty years ago. Today our kids are grown with kids of their own, and our parents are aging, so we spend much of our time praying for our grandkids' schools and friends and spiritual influences, and good health for our parents. Our ministry is also in a different season today, so we have different prayer needs.

That's why we still plan annual vision retreats even after all these years, because we still need guidance and direction. These times away are not something we outgrow as our marriage strengthens. They're times we depend on even more.

Plan for Romance

When it comes to growing a strong and healthy marriage, never underestimate the power of a comfortable, king-sized bed.

Whenever I explain the concept of a vision retreat to couples, I can see the wheels turning. Wives are ecstatic over the idea of sharing their thoughts and feelings, and they often want a detailed list of all the questions they get to ask.

The men, however, have only one thing on their minds. "So, you're saying we'll be all alone and the kids won't be there?" If men were jukeboxes, most would have just one record in the queue.

In this case that's okay, because romance is an important part of a healthy vision retreat. God created us for intimacy, and it's through intimacy that we truly become one flesh. We're wired to desire sex, because in marriage, sex is a sacred, godly act.

When couples begin to feel distant and disenfranchised from each other, it's often because intimacy has taken a backseat to the busyness and worries of life. Coming back together reminds us of how much we need each other to feel complete.

Sex is a stark reminder that there are some needs I have that only Karen can fulfill, and that Karen has needs only I can fulfill. God brought us together for a purpose—to complete each other—and sexual intimacy is one of our deepest and most powerful reminders of that truth.

When preparing for your vision retreat, be creative and intentional. Put effort into creating a romantic atmosphere, almost as if you were planning another honeymoon. See it as an opportunity to court your spouse, because that's exactly what you're doing. You might even plan a few romantic surprises, like taking a special gift or making dinner reservations at a place you've never been. Plan things that you know your spouse will enjoy, then let the sparks fly where they will.

Don't Forget to Have Fun

Beyond all that, the only other advice I have for planning a vision retreat is to have fun and not plan too many activities. Above all else, this is a time for prayer and introspection. A time for taking long walks in the woods, for sitting on the porch and watching the sunset, for holding hands as you cross a river, for sharing your heart and listening as your partner shares theirs. A time to put away your clock and let God direct your day. A time to tell your spouse how much they mean to you and how lost you would be without them.

This is an opportunity to say all the things you've neglected to say and to show your spouse how much you love and respect them.

These are the kinds of moments that make for a strong and vibrant marriage. And any attempt to draw closer to your spouse will be infinitely blessed by God.

7

The Language of Love

Complaints often reveal the key to our spouse's inner longing for emotional love.

Gary Chapman

If we're serious about having meaningful, fulfilling, productive relationships, we can't afford to let inadequate communication skills carry our conversations.

Gary Smalley

One day I was getting dressed for work and decided to wear a new shirt someone had given me. It was a nice-looking shirt, and the size was exactly what I wear—a 16.5-inch neck and a 35-inch sleeve.

I took it out of the package and asked Karen to iron out the creases for me so I could wear it. But when I slipped it on, the shirt didn't fit. It was an Italian cut, and apparently I'm not Italian, because it was snug in all the wrong places. My chest muscles ride a little lower than they used to, so I couldn't get it buttoned in the front. Karen doesn't like me showing off my sexy figure that way, so I changed shirts.

A few days later, I decided to drop by the store and exchange the shirt. It was purchased at a high-end retail shop not far from our house, and I was in the area, so I stopped by.

The guy behind the counter was a nice-enough looking fellow, so I handed him the shirt and explained that I wanted to exchange it for something a bit larger. He unfolded the shirt, held it up in front of him, and said, "This shirt has been worn."

"No, it hasn't," I told him.

"Yes, it has," he said.

"No, it hasn't," I said back.

He looked at it again and said, "Yes, this shirt has been worn. We can't exchange used clothing."

Once again I told him, "No, it hasn't been worn. My wife pressed it for me, but I never wore it."

He still didn't get it. "Yes, this shirt has been worn."

I was starting to get agitated, so I explained it once more, this time a bit slower. "No, the shirt hasn't been worn. My wife pressed it before I tried it on, but then I discovered it didn't fit. I never wore it, and I never washed it. Now I'd like to exchange it for something larger."

He glared at me over the top of his glasses, laid the shirt on the counter, mumbled something under his breath, and went into the back room to get his manager. By this time I was beginning to get really irritated.

A few seconds later they both came back to the counter, and he said to his manager, "This guy wants to return this shirt, but he's already worn it."

He was talking about me in the third person, as if I wasn't even there. The manager didn't look at me either; he just picked up the shirt and held it out in front of him so he could see it in the light. Then he did something I couldn't believe. He started sniffing the armpits! First one and then the other. *Is this guy for real?* I thought.

After thoroughly inspecting and smelling the shirt, he laid it back down and said to the salesman, "Okay, give him another one." Then he turned his nose up in the air and walked away. The whole time he was there, he never once made eye contact. He never even looked in my direction.

Back in my unsaved days, I probably would have dragged those two pretty boys over the counter and whipped them up one escalator and down the other. But Jesus wouldn't like that, so I just bit my tongue and started looking for another shirt.

It was a humiliating experience. I've never felt so judged and belittled by a salesman. You can bet I'll never spend another dime in that store, even though I happen to like a lot of the clothes they sell. I take my business where I'm appreciated.

Poor Communication

It's insulting when a salesman treats you with that kind of contempt. But it's deeply demoralizing when it happens in a marriage. And it's far more common than you might expect.

I didn't walk into the store that day to criticize or get into an argument. I just had a simple problem with a shirt and needed to work it out. When I tried to communicate my needs, I was met with hostility and disrespect.

Too often that same thing happens in marriage. One spouse will have a question or concern, and the other will immediately get defensive. They assume they're about to be attacked, so their guard goes up. And the matter quickly goes from bad to worse.

Whenever I speak or teach on the dynamics of marriage, one of the most common problems I hear about from couples is that they struggle to communicate effectively. They know they are doing something wrong, but they can't figure out what to do about it.

The truth is, almost all arguments in marriage are caused by poor communication. They could be prevented if we could just figure out how to talk to each other in a healthy and productive way. The enemy knows this, and he works tirelessly to discourage and frustrate us by breaking down our lines of communication. If he can keep us from communicating, he can keep our marriage in a constant state of confusion. When we can't talk to each other, we begin to feel distant and detached and neglected, and when that happens, intimacy goes out the window.

Communication is the lifeblood of a relationship. It's how two souls connect. It's how two individual people learn to become one flesh. It's how thoughts and feelings and dreams are transferred from one person to another. Without communication, a marriage relationship becomes nothing more than a living arrangement. And *how* we communicate is just as important as *what* we communicate.

A Happy Customer

Let me tell you about an entirely different experience I had in a different department store. On this occasion I was having a problem with a leather jacket I had purchased a couple of years earlier. The shoulder stitches were starting to wear, and it was my favorite leather jacket, so I took it back to the store to see if I could get it repaired.

I was greeted at the counter by a pleasant young woman, and I explained my problem to her. I showed her the jacket and asked, "Do you think you could send that off somewhere and get it fixed?"

She smiled and said, "Of course we can. I'm happy to do that for you." She took out a tag and began filling it out.

I was thrilled that it was that easy. I was afraid I might have to search out a tailor in town to fix it for me.

She was halfway finished filling out the tag when she suddenly stopped and put her pen down. She looked at me and said, "You don't want to do this."

"Really?" I said.

"No, you want a new one," she said.

I thought she was about to try to sell me a new jacket. But before I had a chance to respond, she said, "Go over to the rack and pick out a new jacket."

"You mean for free?" I asked.

"Sure," she answered. "This shouldn't have come loose. There's something wrong with this jacket, so go get yourself a new one."

I was a bit taken aback. "No, that's okay," I told her. "I've already had this one for a couple of years, and I've worn it quite a bit. I don't mind just getting it fixed."

But she was adamant. "This should have lasted a lot longer than that. You need a new jacket. Go pick out one and we'll exchange it."

I was shocked, but I wasn't going to argue. I went to the rack and found another jacket I liked. It was more expensive than the one I had, but I was happy to pay the difference when I took it to the counter.

When she scanned the tag, the price difference was just over a hundred dollars, so I pulled out my wallet.

"No, don't worry about it," she said.

"Are you sure?" I asked. "Because I'm happy to pay the difference."

"No, you've gone through enough trouble already," she said. "We'll take care of the difference. You have a wonderful day."

I walked out of that store beaming with satisfaction. I couldn't believe the good customer service they had. And I've been back there numerous times since that day. I love shopping there, because I know if I ever have a problem, they'll take care of it.

A Customer Service Counter

Successful stores understand how important it is to communicate with their customers. They give them the right to complain and voice concerns. They set up a customer service counter right in the front of the store, and they welcome feedback. They gladly handle problems when they arise. You feel safe shopping there, because you know they care about what you think. And if you ever have a concern, they'll jump through hoops to make it right.

That's how it should be in marriage. All the best marriages have customer service counters. Spouses say to each other, "If you ever have a problem, don't be afraid to talk to me about it. If I ever do anything to offend you, please tell me. If I'm not treating you the way I should, you can feel safe coming to me. I promise I won't get defensive. And I won't turn you away. We'll find a way to work it out."

A hallmark feature of every great marriage is that couples allow each other the freedom to complain. They encourage open and honest communication with no strings attached, no concerns of retribution, no fear of ridicule or rejection. The customer service counter is always open.

All the best marriages are built on healthy communication. The better couples communicate, the stronger and more vibrant their marriage becomes.

As a pastor and counselor, I've seen countless couples restore their broken and battered marriages simply by learning the art of good communication. When struggling couples come to me for help, this is the first area I target. Healing can't begin until couples learn to talk to each other with respect and dignity and honesty.

That's why vision retreats are such a critical part of our counseling ministry. They open up lines of communication and teach couples how to speak freely with each other. At a vision retreat, the customer service counter is open for business and ready to make things right.

But for communication to work, you have to abide by the rules. Like with any skill in marriage, there's both a right way and a wrong way to communicate. Poor communication can destroy a marriage, while healthy communication can strengthen and stabilize it.

Through the years I've identified what I believe to be the five most critical skills of healthy communication. These are five things that must be present for communication to work properly—five attitudes that need to be kept in check at all times if your customer service counter is going to make your most important customer happy.

Skill #1: A Caring Tone

I've often said that if God hadn't called me into the ministry, I probably would have been a lawyer, because I can argue my way out of a gang fight—and probably go home with all the knives as a bonus. My tongue often works faster than my brain, which is a great skill for a debate team but a terrible habit to take into marriage. I had a horrible time controlling my tongue, and it caused a lot of problems in the early years of our marriage.

Many times Karen would try to communicate a problem to me, and I would immediately begin to argue. I would discount her concerns and use the chance to lecture her on why she was wrong. I was far more interested in winning the argument than trying to understand her side of the story. I was a pro at communicating my thoughts, but I knew almost nothing about listening.

After God stepped in and began restoring our marriage, I knew this was one area of my life that had to change. So I worked hard at learning to control my tongue. It was one of the toughest battles of my life, but I knew I had to conquer my compulsion to always be right if our marriage was ever going to work.

With God's help, I did get better. Much better. But old habits die hard, and even when I thought I had mastered the art of communicating, I still had a problem with my tone. I was sincerely listening to Karen and trying to work things out, but the way I talked to her said otherwise. Though my words were genuine, my tone communicated only frustration.

Several times Karen said to me, "Jimmy, I wish I could record the way you talk to me, then you'd see why I don't feel like you're listening."

I honestly thought I was doing a good job communicating, so I'd say to her, "You're wrong, Karen. I do care. And I am listening." But she never bought it. I was thoroughly convinced that she was simply being hypercritical.

Then one morning during my quiet time with the Lord, I was praying and meditating on Ephesians 5. I was reading the section of Scripture where husbands are commanded to love their wives as Christ loves the church, and I got to verse 26, which says, "to make her holy, cleansing her by the washing with water through the word." Just as I read the passage, God gave me two powerful visions.

The first vision was a scene of Jesus washing me with water. He and I were standing side by side with a bowl between us. Jesus was gently scooping handfuls of water out of the bowl and pouring it over my head. His eyes were patient and kind, and he continued to fill his hands with water and pour it over me.

I began reflecting on how long I'd been saved, and I thought, *Jesus is still washing me all these years later. He is still working on cleansing my heart. I still have so many issues he needs to deal with, but he never gets impatient. He just keeps pouring, keeps bathing, keeps ministering to my needs.*

Then suddenly I got a second vision. This scene was of Karen and me, and it was just as vivid and surreal as the first one, but completely different. Karen was standing in front of me, and I had a fire hose in my hand. The water was turned on full blast, and I was washing her down. She was turned to one side, cowering beneath the force of the water.

I began to pray, *Lord, is that what I do? Is that how I treat Karen? Is that the way I try to wash her?*

77

Those two visions forever changed the way I responded to Karen. For the first time, I finally understood what she had been trying to tell me. I may have been speaking truth and even meant it in a loving way, but my tone was far too forceful. I still hadn't learned how to communicate gently and softly, with a loving and caring demeanor.

God convicted my spirit in a powerful way. And I promised him that morning that I would do better.

The very next day I had an issue I needed to talk to Karen about, and I didn't want to put it off, but I also was committed to changing the way I talked to her.

Usually when I had something to talk to Karen about, I would take her aside and share my concerns, then I'd say to her, "Do you understand what I'm saying? Are you sure you understand?"

She'd say, "Yes, I heard you, Jimmy."

But I couldn't leave it alone. The lawyer in me wanted to make sure I had communicated my point effectively. So I'd tell her again and then say, "I just want to make sure we're on the same page here. Are you sure you understand?"

That was my regular way of communicating with Karen. I had to make sure I got my point across. But this time I wasn't going to do that.

Karen was in the kitchen, and I walked in and said, "Karen, I just wanted to share something with you." I gently told her what was on my mind, kissed her on the cheek, thanked her for listening, and went back into the den. I honestly had to fight the urge to repeat it several times, since that was my usual habit, but I was committed to changing the way I communicated.

I continued that practice over the next few days. Each time I talked to Karen, I'd quietly say what I needed to and then let the matter drop. In my mind I was forming new habits, but it never occurred to me that Karen would even notice. Then one day she came to me and said, "Jimmy, I've noticed the kind way you've been talking to me the last few days, and I really appreciate it. You don't know how much that means to me."

It confirmed for me just how much my tone must have been bothering her. I hadn't even realized I was doing it, but the minute I changed, she noticed a marked difference.

How we communicate is just as important as what we're trying to say. A loving and caring tone is the first and most critical step when learning how to effectively communicate with your spouse.

Skill #2: Frequent Communication

Healthy communication is also a daily practice. To build an open and honest relationship, you have to talk often and intentionally. This involves planning regular times throughout the day to communicate and share your feelings.

When our kids were young, Karen and I developed a regular ritual at bedtime. We would begin early getting the kids ready for bed, then we'd spend some time in their bedrooms praying with them and tucking them in. Often I'd get out my guitar and we'd sing a few worship songs. Once we got them settled in and kissed them good night, they understood that they weren't allowed to come out of their rooms. They could read if they wanted, but they couldn't talk and they couldn't get up. They knew that this was Mommy and Daddy's time to be alone.

Then Karen and I would retreat to our bedroom. We had a small sitting area in the corner, and we would sit and visit. Usually we'd have a bowl of fresh popcorn to share, and we'd talk for as long as we wanted. If there was something on television we wanted to watch, we'd tape it for later, because this was our sacred time together.

When we first started doing this, I wondered what we would find to talk about, since we'd been talking off and on all day long, but that was never a problem. Once we got started, we never seemed to run out of things to say. The only problem we had was making ourselves stop talking so we could get some sleep. Honestly, I think I enjoyed it as much as Karen. I actually had to teach myself how to communicate with Karen, but once I learned, it became the highlight of my day.

When the kids got old enough to stay in the house alone, we started taking walks around the block each morning so we could get some exercise while we talked. We'd walk for an hour and a half and use the time to visit. Usually we would talk for forty-five minutes, then pray for the remaining forty-five minutes. I can still remember so many of the prayers we lifted up during our walks together and the powerful ways God answered those prayers.

Today we have an empty nest, and we spend most of our days together, but our nightly talks are still sacred to us. Every night we still sit together and visit. And we leave the television off until we're finished visiting.

All these years later, we still never run out of things to talk about. And that time is still my favorite part of each day.

If you haven't made the effort to set aside a regular time to communicate with your spouse, I encourage you to start doing that right away. Schedule a time and place to visit for at least thirty to sixty minutes each day. Taking a walk together is a great way to start. If you can't do that, make yourself turn off the television, cell phones, and computers each night until you've had a chance to visit. Whatever it takes to get you and your spouse talking face-to-face on a daily basis is worth the effort.

Skill #3: Intimate Communication

Remember the ways you and your spouse used to hug and cuddle and touch before you were married? Remember the pet names you used to use, the sweet nothings you whispered into each other's ears, the way you would hold hands as you walked through the park? Remember the way you used to gaze into each other's eyes?

These little acts of affection are the things that drew your hearts together, because they communicated value and closeness. It was your way of letting each other know how much you cared and how loyal you were to the relationship.

When marriages begin to struggle, these intimate moments are the first things to go. We stop showing affection because we no longer feel affectionate. We withdraw physically as well as emotionally. We no longer hold hands or whisper sweet nothings, and romantic gazes become a thing of the past.

But relationships can't survive without intimate touch and affection. These little acts of intimacy are critical to keeping a marriage from becoming stale and boring. It's our way of saying to our spouse, "I'm still attracted to you. I care deeply for you. I'm still invested in this relationship. You are the only one for me."

It is through intimate touch that we build our mate's self-esteem and reaffirm our love and commitment. And physical intimacy doesn't always have to be sexual.

If you saw Karen and me throughout the day, you'd likely get nauseous, because when we're alone we act like a couple of googly-eyed schoolkids. She will be walking into the kitchen, minding her own business, and I'll sneak up from behind and grab her around the waist. I'll give her a big hug and kiss and say, "I love you." Then we'll both go about our business.

When I see her sitting on the couch reading, I'll snuggle in next to her and whisper something sweet in her ear. We'll exchange a few knowing glances, then I'll go on my way.

And she does the same with me. Often I'll be getting dressed in the morning and she'll pinch me on the behind or grab me and give me a big kiss. I'll be sitting in a chair after a long day at work, and she'll sneak up behind me and massage my shoulders. Then she'll wrap her arms around my neck and kiss me on the ear.

Throughout the day we look for ways to show nonsexual affection to each other, because this is the best way we know to communicate our love. We're constantly touching and hugging, speaking kind and caring words, communicating value and affection to each other. These little acts of intimacy have done wonders to strengthen our relationship.

Skill #4: Honest Communication

The fourth critical skill of effective communication is creating an atmosphere of openness and honesty. You have to give your partner permission to come to you with any question or complaint, no matter how sensitive it might be, and to talk to you without fear or intimidation. You should have that same right with them.

Often when I counsel people who are struggling in their marriage, they will open up to me about some issues that are deeply affecting their relationship. I will ask them, "Have you talked to your spouse about this?"

Immediately they will say something like, "Oh no. I could never talk to him about this. He would be furious."

Oprah Winfrey has been known to say, "You train people how to treat you," and she's absolutely right. But that's not always a good thing. In marriage, people learn quickly what they can and can't say to their spouse, and it creates a tremendous amount of tension and insecurity.

Wives learn which issues are hot-button issues, and they steer clear of those topics. Otherwise their husbands might fly off the handle.

Husbands also learn not to bring up certain sensitive subjects with their wives to keep them from withdrawing emotionally or withholding sex.

We train our partners which issues are safe for conversation and which ones are not, and we fear being punished if we ever cross those lines. But that's extremely unhealthy, and it creates walls of tension within the marriage. And walls within a relationship are toxic and destructive.

Healthy communication is always open and honest and safe. It is completely free of walls, hot buttons, or sensitive issues. It is saying to your spouse, "No topic is off-limits. You can tell me anything, and I promise not to hold it against you."

Healthy marriages not only allow honesty but encourage it. They expect it. They seek it out.

If I ever think that something might be bothering Karen, I will sit down next to her and say, "Please tell me if I've done something to upset you. I really want to know." Karen knows that I am her safe place and that I care deeply about her feelings. She knows that she can come to me about anything that's on her mind, no matter how large or small a matter it might be, and that I will listen without judging or belittling her. I will always take her comments to heart and never respond harshly. And I feel that same freedom with her.

The Bible tells us to speak the truth in love, because truth is crucial to any healthy relationship, but truth without love is cruel. Truth for the sake of truth is usually hurtful and insensitive. For truth to build closeness and intimacy, it must be couched in love and tenderness and affection. It can never be a source of vengeance or retribution.

Karen knows that I would never hurt her feelings on purpose, but there are times when I'll say or do something that upsets her. When that happens, she knows that I want her to tell me about it. When she does, she doesn't attack me personally. She will say something like, "Jimmy, when we were running late yesterday and you were asking me to hurry, I know you weren't trying to be harsh, but it hurt my feelings a little. I'm sure you weren't trying to sound angry, but that's how I took it, and I just wanted to let you know that."

Her words are honest and truthful but not meant as a personal attack. And I don't take them that way.

This is what it means to speak the truth in love. It means learning to be honest without attacking or hurting each other. It means thinking about your words before speaking them. It means checking your motives before speaking your mind.

Skill #5: A Team Spirit

When Karen and I first married, we quickly learned that money was going to be our greatest source of tension. From the first day of our marriage, we fought about our finances. They were a constant source of struggle with us.

To me, money is a source of fun and enjoyment. I love spending and giving and using money to bless other people. Whenever I got a paycheck, I was ready to go out and have a good time.

But to Karen, money is a means to security. Karen is a very generous person, but she's also very sensible and pragmatic. Saving for a rainy day is important to her and critical to her sense of safety.

We have completely different languages when it comes to money, and it caused tremendous friction between us.

Almost all couples have subjects that become sources of conflict. For some it might be parenting issues, problems with in-laws, or career decisions. A wife may want to stay home with the kids while her husband wants her to work. A husband may want to live in one city while his wife wants to live in another. There are always disagreements within the relationship, and sometimes these disagreements become toxic.

For communication to work in marriage, there has to be a team spirit. When an issue comes around that causes conflict, you have to find a way to resolve it. Agreeing to disagree may sound like a good solution, but it's not. That's simply agreeing to ignore a problem until it becomes fatal. You have to find a workable solution, even if it means one party needs to defer their will to the other.

For Karen and me, this meant sitting down and hashing out a budget that we could both live with. It was a budget that gave me the freedom to have fun and spend a reasonable portion of our income on things that Karen might consider frivolous, while putting away enough each month to make Karen feel secure. It was a workable compromise and soon became a nonnegotiable part of our marriage. We worked out a win-win solution, and it put an end to the conflict.

Another hot-button issue in the early years of our marriage involved my driving habits. I was born with a lead foot and a bucketful of testosterone, so I drove much faster than I should have. This was a terrible source of anxiety for Karen, and every time we got into the car, we'd start to argue.

I finally realized that the only way we were ever going to get along in the car was for me to slow down and control my need for speed. So that's what I did. In this case there was no compromise to be found, so I simply had to defer my will to hers. But it was the only workable solution, so I made the needed sacrifices.

Dr. Phil often says, "You can either be right or you can be happy," and in this case I decided I'd rather be happy.

Karen and I are a team, and sometimes one player has to take one for the team in order to win. A lot of issues in marriage can't be solved with compromise. When one partner wants to live in Seattle and the other likes Dallas, you have to sit down and make a decision. One spouse has to yield to the other because compromise is impossible.

In those cases, once the decision has been made, the matter needs to be dropped for good. Otherwise it can grow into a constant source of unresolved conflict.

A team spirit is critical to the success of a marriage. And it takes healthy communication for a team to work effectively.

The Counter Is Open

I've often thought about posting a huge sign above our bed that says "Customer Service Counter," because Karen and I have a marriage that is committed to service and honesty and healthy communication. We know there is no issue that can't be resolved by simply talking it through. There is no source of conflict that can't be fixed through loving and honest communication. We are committed to having the best marriage we can possibly create, and that takes an attitude of service and devotion.

In our marriage, the customer service counter is always open and ready to make things right. No one will ever be turned away or disrespected. No complaint will ever be questioned or discounted. No concern will ever be snubbed. No question will ever be refused.

No one will ever sniff your armpits to see if you're telling the truth.

Our marriage is a place of complete safety. If Karen ever gets a "bad jacket," she knows I will say to her, "Just go over to the rack and get yourself a new one, because I'm here to make you happy."

My goal in this marriage is to make sure I'm the only store she ever wants to shop in. I'll do whatever it takes to keep her coming back for more. She'll never be tempted to shop anywhere else.

And her store is the only one that gets my juices flowing. She knows she has a customer for life, because I've never had a problem in our marriage that she couldn't solve.

Communication is the language of love. It is how you build a strong marriage and then keep that marriage from getting old and stale and tired. It's how you create a love affair that will last a lifetime.

8

Great Marriages Run in Packs

We human beings can survive the most difficult of circumstances if we are not forced to stand alone.

James Dobson

Do not be misled: "Bad company corrupts good character."

1 Corinthians 15:33

Karen and I have been married nearly forty years, and in that time we've had close relationships with at least fifty other couples. I know that's true, because recently I sat down and made a list, just out of curiosity. Obviously, these aren't the only friends we've had through the years, but they're the ones we consider close personal friends—people we hang out with and actually allow into our inner circle of friendship.

Out of all those friends, only one couple has divorced. That's extraordinary when you consider that half of all marriages don't last.

Karen and I are very careful about the friends we choose. We learned years ago how important it is to pick our friends and not let others pick us. We choose friends who share our values and priorities.

The two people who did divorce were actually two of our closest friends. In fact, early in my walk with Christ, the husband had a greater impact on me than any friend I'd ever had. He was a deeply committed man of God, and I loved him dearly. But all that changed when he took a job in another city and moved his family away.

The man who'd hired him was an ungodly man. I could tell by the way he talked that he wasn't a believer. And though our friends found a new church to attend, they never really plugged in because of the husband's busy work schedule. His new job involved a lot of travel, and his boss almost always traveled with him. It was a formula for danger, and I called my friend just a few months into his move to tell him so. I told him my concerns about his ungodly boss, his busy travel schedule, and his lack of involvement in their church, but he didn't listen.

We had very little contact with the couple over the ensuing months, until one weekend when they came to visit. We had them over for dinner and had a fun evening, but something about it didn't feel right. He seemed much more distant and guarded than usual. I could tell his new job and his lack of Christian fellowship were having a negative impact on his life.

Karen noticed it as well. Right after they left, she said to me, "I don't like the way he looks at me. I just feel uncomfortable around him." She couldn't put her finger on it, but she just knew in her spirit that something about him was different.

Less than three weeks later, I got a call from his wife in the middle of the afternoon. She was crying and frantic and could hardly talk. I asked her what was wrong. "He's leaving me," she said, barely able to get out the words. I could hear their children crying in the background. One of them was saying, "Daddy, please don't leave. Don't leave, Daddy!" It was a heart-wrenching sound.

I asked her to let me talk to him, and he reluctantly came to the phone. "Tell me what's going on," I said.

"I'm leaving, Jimmy. And don't try to talk me out of it. I'm moving in with a friend from work."

I asked him why, and he said, "She doesn't give me enough sex." I was stunned by how cold and callous his voice sounded.

"Listen, you have a wonderful, beautiful wife," I told him. "It's wrong of you to do this."

"I know she's a good wife," he said, "but I'm just not happy with our sex life. She's never given me enough sex."

At that instant I knew in my spirit that he had gotten involved in pornography. I'd suspected it for months but never had it confirmed so clearly.

I said to him, "I know what you and your friends do when you travel for work. I know you've been watching pornography in your hotel rooms and going to clubs on the road. I know the filth you've allowed into your mind, and it's not right. What you're doing is wrong. I want you to stay there and wait for me, because you and I need to talk."

Through the entire conversation I could hear his precious little children pleading with their father to stay. But it was too late. He said he would be gone before I got there, and the minute he hung up the phone, he walked out the door for good.

That happened over twenty years ago, and the event still haunts me.

The Power of Peer Pressure

There is no overstating the power that peer pressure plays in a person's life. And peer pressure works both ways—it can be negative or positive.

As parents, we all know how critical it is to help our kids connect with the right kinds of friends because friends have an incredible influence over their lives. We can do everything right as parents and still lose the battle if our kids fall in with the wrong crowd. We can take our kids to church, teach them right from wrong, pray with them night and day, and ingrain our values into their minds, but all of that can fall by the wayside through the influence of one ungodly friend.

I know kids who grew up in devout, righteous households with wonderful, loving parents, who went completely astray by allowing themselves to make friends with the wrong person. Today they are making choices that will forever affect the direction of their lives.

The effects of some of those choices may be irreparable. I pray that they'll eventually come back to their roots and embrace their parents' values, but in the meantime, a lot of bad seed is being sown, and they are sure to reap negative consequences because of it.

If you want to see a person's future, just look at their friends. You always become whom you hang out with. It is a law of the universe. If you allow evil and immoral friends into your life, you will eventually find yourself engaged in evil and immoral behavior.

Before Karen and I married, I had immoral friends, and we did everything together. I went to church just about every week, but even at church I gravitated toward the worst kids. I was a bad kid, and my friends reflected that truth.

Karen didn't like my friends, and several times she asked me to stop hanging out with them, but that only made me angry. "Don't ask me to give up my friends," I told her, "because that's not going to happen. I love you, but I also like my friends, and I'm sticking with them." I knew they were a bad influence, but I didn't really care. Loyalty was a big issue with me, and I would never turn my back on a buddy.

At least that's what I thought at the time. When Jesus came into my life and saved me, the first thing he ever spoke into my spirit was to cut ties with my ungodly friends. It was one of the hardest things he could have asked me to do, but the conviction in my spirit was unmistakable. I knew that God wanted me to completely sever the relationships I had with unbelieving, unrighteous friends.

I obeyed God, but I didn't like it. Before that time I had always had running buddies to do things with, and suddenly I had no male friends to hang out with. I was lonely and irritable, and Karen usually caught the brunt of my frustration.

Karen and I attended different churches when we were dating, but after we married we decided to find a new church together. I didn't like any of the churches we visited because I honestly couldn't relate to Christian men. They all seemed boring and plastic to me. I missed my old friendships and had a hard time making new friends.

Then one day we finally found a church we both liked, and we immediately plugged into a class of young married couples. The class was taught by an older couple I really liked. Their names were Kerm and Lou Ethel Albertson.

Kerm and Lou Ethel had a wonderful marriage, and Karen and I began to look to them as mentors. I was still a terrible husband and a long way from where God wanted me to be, but somehow I found myself gravitating toward them.

When I saw the way they treated each other, the way they looked at each other, the way they held hands as they walked—even after many years of marriage—I started wondering what they had that Karen and I seemed to be missing. Their relationship was completely foreign to me, but it was infectious just the same. I desperately wanted what they had.

A Common Bond

For almost two years, Karen and I attended the Albertsons' class, and in that time we became good friends with them. They were the main reason we never missed church. We always looked forward to seeing them and often hung out after class to visit.

One day Karen and I had a huge fight. I can't remember what it was about, only that it lasted for hours. And as usual, I said things I knew I shouldn't have said. That afternoon Karen told me to get dressed for dinner because the Albertsons had asked us to go out to dinner with them.

"Tonight?" I asked her. "When did you arrange that?"

"Just now," she told me. "I called and told them we were fighting, and they asked us to go out for dinner."

That made me furious. I couldn't believe Karen would tell on me like that, and I almost made her go alone. But I was already embarrassed, so I decided to go and make the best of it. I figured I could put on my best smile and downplay the argument so they wouldn't think that I was a total jerk.

That night was the most awkward dinner I'd ever had. It was obvious to everyone that Karen and I were having a hard time in our marriage, and I hated feeling like the bad guy, even though I was. Kerm and Lou Ethel were incredibly gracious and pretended not to notice the wall that Karen and I had erected between us.

Then after dinner, something interesting happened. As we visited over cake and coffee, Kerm began telling us stories about the early years of their marriage. He told us how immature they both were when they married and how hard a time they had getting along. He told us several stories about arguments they'd had and how they often wouldn't talk to each other for days on end. He said they used to fight over the smallest things, and at times they wondered if their marriage would even survive.

I was speechless. I couldn't imagine seeing them argue, much less getting into fights that were just as bitter as the ones Karen and I had. Somehow I had assumed they were "soul mates" and just naturally got along.

Karen and I didn't say much on the ride home that evening, but I knew we were both thinking the same thing. *If they can get past what they went through and come out this much in love, maybe there's still hope for us.*

Though we were still angry with each other, we both felt a strange sense of relief. And encouragement. We knew we had a long way to go and a lot of maturing to do, but something about the evening made an indelible impact on our hearts.

Maybe, we thought, *just maybe, if we stick with it, someday we can have a marriage like theirs.*

The Power of Community

The writer of Hebrews tells us, "And let us consider how we may spur one another on toward love and good deeds, not giving up meeting together, as some are in the habit of doing, but encouraging one another—and all the more as you see the Day approaching" (10:24–25).

There is a reason Christians are told to bind their hearts and lives with other committed followers. We're commanded to stick together, to find people of like mind and spur each other on "toward love and good deeds," and to meet together regularly so we can encourage each other to stay the course.

People need community to survive. We need to be around people who think like we do, who share our values, who understand our struggles, who have been through what we're going through. We need people who can say to us, "You can do this," "I know you can make it," and "I believe in you." It's through community that weak people become strong, and strong people become even stronger.

I've been a believer for nearly forty years, yet I'm convinced that I could not survive without the fellowship of other believers. If I had to cut ties with all my Christian friends and instead live only among ungodly, unrighteous people, I would find myself struggling to remain faithful. The same is true for you.

We all are affected deeply by peer pressure, both good and bad.

One of the primary reasons Karen and I have a strong and healthy marriage is that we decided years ago to surround ourselves with the right kinds of people. When God stepped in and saved our marriage, he began bringing couples into our lives to set an example for us. People who saw the struggles we were going through and who were committed to guiding and encouraging us as we navigated the inevitable storms of marriage. People who had weathered the same gale-force winds and could serve as a beacon of light, showing us which way to go. People like the Albertsons, who were willing to take us aside and speak into our lives, helping us get where God wanted to take us.

If you've found yourself struggling in your marriage, I encourage you to take a long, hard look at the people you've allowed into your life. Look at your friends and acquaintances—the people you hang out with at church, your friends in the neighborhood, your co-workers, the couples you get together with on a regular basis. Are they the kind of people you want to emulate? Do they have the kind of marriage you want to have? Do they treat each other with love and respect? Do they hold themselves to godly standards of living? Do they influence your relationship for good?

These are critical questions that need to be dealt with honestly, because the people you hang out with have an overwhelming impact on the health of your marriage.

The friends Karen and I have in our lives are not by accident or default. We've allowed them in for a reason. Our friendships are intentional and chosen with great care. We pray about our friendships and have no problem cutting ties with people who drag us down as a couple. Our marriage is far too important to us to think or do otherwise.

And our friends don't believe in divorce. It is simply not an option for them, no matter how difficult things may get. They are committed to staying together, and nothing would convince them otherwise.

I often joke that if I ever threatened to leave Karen, my buddies would get together and drag me behind the woodshed to convince me otherwise. Anyone from Texas can tell you that nothing good ever happens behind a woodshed.

That's why I call these guys my buddies. They hold me accountable. They won't allow my sinful nature to get the best of me. They spur me on toward the good and encourage me to stay the course. And I do the same for them.

Those are the kinds of friendships that every couple needs. If you don't have those in your life, you need to find them. You need to have a strong, godly support system in your life, a life-giving church to attend, a group of friends who will lift you up and hold you accountable. You need people around you who will call you on the carpet when you make poor choices, who will come alongside you when times get tough, who understand your struggles and are willing to help you through them, who know your hopes and dreams, and who share your value system. You need friends who will hold you to your word and keep you on the right track in your marriage.

Bad company corrupts good character. Good company has the opposite effect. It strengthens character and builds resolve. That's why whenever you see a great marriage, you can be sure there's a pack of other great marriages right behind it.

9

The Gardener and the Cheerleader

Husbands, love your wives, just as Christ loved the church.

Ephesians 5:25

The wife must respect her husband.

Ephesians 5:33

What would you say is the biggest crisis facing our country at the moment?

Ask that question at a party and you'll be amazed at the different answers you'll get. Some might talk about the size of government or political ideologies. Others may say it's the broken school system, big labor unions, or self-serving politicians. Still others might bring up the lack of jobs, plunging real estate prices, or the collapsing currency. Chances are you'll start a debate that will go on long after the party ends, because everyone has an opinion, and there's definitely no shortage of crises these days.

My answer might surprise you. I think the biggest crisis facing us is the large and rising number of people choosing to cohabitate instead of getting married. We used to call it "shacking up," but I guess that sounded too sinful, so now it's called *cohabitation*. But it's the same thing, and it's a huge problem. It's a profound indication of just how far the family unit has broken down through the years. And when the family unit breaks down, cultures are thrown into chaos. In fact, almost every societal problem you can think of has its roots in this one overarching crisis. Families are the foundation of society, and when they lose their way, society starts to crumble.

Divorce has become such a predominant part of our culture that it's almost expected. So people started believing that the best approach is to simply move in together. It's not that they're afraid of getting married. What they're afraid of is getting divorced.

I recently heard about a survey in which 93 percent of those polled admitted that having a stable, lifelong marriage was "very important" to them. Yet in a follow-up question, less than half of that number believed that having a happy marriage was possible to attain.

People haven't lost the dream of marriage. They've simply lost hope in that dream.

The Ephesians 5 Model

Marriage is anything but hopeless. Marriage was created by God, and he is a God of hope and abundance. He designed marriage to be an infinitely rewarding and fulfilling experience, not to be frustrating and confusing. And he didn't leave it to chance. God gave us the perfect formula for a happy and productive marriage in the pages of Scripture. It's a formula that doesn't take any special skills or abilities to comprehend. It isn't hard to decipher or difficult to understand. It certainly doesn't take a Bible scholar to interpret. It's a simple plan that reveals for us the secret to a marriage that is filled with hope and purpose and is certifiably indestructible.

What it does take is a willing heart and a humble spirit.

This plan is laid out for us in the fifth chapter of Ephesians. I referred to this section of Scripture earlier, but a passage with this much power deserves repeating:

Submit to one another out of reverence for Christ.

Wives, submit yourselves to your own husbands as you do to the Lord. For the husband is the head of the wife as Christ is the head of the church. . . . Now as the church submits to Christ, so also wives should submit to their husbands in everything.

Husbands, love your wives, just as Christ loved the church and gave himself up for her. . . . In this same way, husbands ought to love their wives as their own bodies. He who loves his wife loves himself. After all, no one ever hated their own body, but they feed and care for their body, just as Christ does the church. . . . Each one of you also must love his wife as he loves himself, and the wife must respect her husband.

verses 21–25, 28–29, 33

As a counselor, I often read this passage aloud to couples, and I almost always get the same response. The husbands love the part about their wives submitting to them. In fact, most can quote that section by heart. But they get really quiet when Paul outlines how they should act toward their wives. Not many men are ready to be held to such a high standard.

The women have the opposite response. They love what Paul has to say about husbands being sacrificial and sensitive and nourishing, but they often cringe at the thought of being submissive.

These reactions don't surprise me. In fact, they're perfectly predictable, given the countercultural nature of the passage. Everything about our society tells us to guard our independence, to look after ourselves, to seek what will meet our own needs and not let anyone get in our way. But God tells us the exact opposite.

Society tells us marriage is about finding the right person. God tells us marriage is about *being* the right kind of person.

Culture tells us marriage is about meeting our own needs while maintaining our own identity. God tells us marriage is about sacrificing our needs for the sake of our spouse.

The world tells us marriage is about happiness. God tells us marriage is about holiness.

In God's economy, things are seldom as they seem. God tells us if you want to find yourself, you do it by losing yourself in service to others. It's in losing yourself that you find true contentment and joy.

Nowhere is that dynamic truer than within the covenant of marriage.

Love and Respect

In the Ephesians 5 model of marriage, women are told, "Submit yourselves to your own husbands as you do to the Lord" (v. 22). Many women today recoil at the thought of submitting, but only because we've misconstrued what it means to submit.

When we submit ourselves to Jesus, we don't fear being dominated or controlled or abused. What we're doing is giving him a place of honor and respect and leadership in our lives. We know the character of Jesus, and it's in that character we place our trust.

It is in this same spirit of humility that women are told to submit to their husbands. To hold them in a place of honor and respect and leadership. Not to become subservient or allow themselves to be abused but to treat their husbands with admiration and esteem.

I'm aware that this is not an easy thing to do, especially with husbands who have done little to deserve their wives' respect. Many women are quick to point out, "If I gave my husband that kind of honor, all it would do is encourage him to keep being bad!" Most of their time is spent nagging and complaining because they want to discourage irresponsible behavior. One wife said to me, "If he ever starts acting like Jesus, I'll be happy to treat him like Jesus." Women are afraid of giving respect to a man who doesn't deserve it, because it just might make things worse.

And husbands often have the same kinds of fears. When Karen and I first married, I was a horrible brute and tried to dominate her, but only because I was afraid of losing control. I knew from Scripture that I was supposed to serve her the way Christ serves the church, but I was convinced that if I ever started doing that, she would take advantage of it. I imagined myself walking around the house in an apron, vacuuming and doing the dishes, thinking, *How did this happen?*

Whenever I explain the Ephesians 5 model to couples, neither wants to be the first to change their behavior. A natural defense mechanism kicks in, and they immediately become hesitant and fearful.

But one thing I've never seen in the passage is a disclaimer. God never tells wives to submit to their husbands only when they deserve it. He never tells husbands to be loving and sacrificial after they get the respect they need.

The Christian life isn't about reacting to others based on their behavior. It's about responding to others according to the principles of Scripture, regardless of how we're treated. You and I are called to a higher standard of behavior. As Christians, we commit to being imitators of Christ. To turn the other cheek when we've been wronged. To treat others as we would have them treat us. To put the needs of others above our own needs. To be salt and light, even in the midst of darkness.

You and I are called to live according to our faith, regardless of our circumstances and what those around us choose to do. The Ephesians 5 model of marriage is an extension of that calling. We respond to our mate based on the principles God set before us, regardless of how our mate responds.

In my years of counseling couples, I've encouraged countless husbands and wives to swallow their pride and be the first to start treating their mates the way God outlined in the Ephesians 5 model. When they do, I almost always see a miracle happen in their relationship.

When a husband steps out in faith and begins loving and nurturing his wife the way God intended, the wife starts to soften. Before long she is treating him with the respect and dignity he always longed for. She begins submitting to his leadership and trusting him to make wise choices.

When a wife takes the initiative and starts treating her husband with respect and honor, he starts living up to her expectations. He begins leading with integrity and character. He starts to become the man she longs to have.

This isn't always the case, but I've seen it more often than not. When God's people start to live in obedience to his Word, miracles start to happen.

Why This Is God's Perfect Plan

I'm convinced that whenever you see a great marriage, what you're seeing is a couple living out the Ephesians 5 model. There is really no other way to do it. You will never find two self-serving, self-involved people growing a healthy and productive relationship with each other. Even if they seem happy on the surface, you can bet anger and resentment are brewing below. Marriage was designed as a covenant of service and self-sacrifice between two people, and any other model is destined for failure or, at the very least, a lifelong battle and frustration.

Let me outline for you three reasons why the Ephesians 5 model is such a perfect plan for marriage.

1. It Gives the Key to Lifelong Attraction

Just as moths gravitate toward the light, you and I gravitate toward things that attract us. The Ephesians 5 model outlines for both men and women how to remain completely irresistible to each other, even as our bodies start to sag and our hair starts to thin.

Today I can stand in a roomful of male models—each one sickeningly tanned and flat bellied—and be completely confident that I'm the one Karen notices. Not because I'm such a stud, but because I'm the only one in the room who has made it my full-time job to meet her needs and make her happy.

In the same way, Karen will always be my own private supermodel. There's not a woman on the planet who can ever compare, because Karen has thrown all her energies into being my number one fan and cheerleader.

What could possibly be more attractive than that?

Back in high school I used to play football, and if there's one universal truth about football players, it's that they love their cheerleaders. Not just because they're cute, but because it's their job to cheer the players on. They stand on the sidelines in their coordinated little outfits, continually shouting words of encouragement. "Come on, you can do it!" they yell.

Even when things start to turn bad, they remain positive, cheering words of support. "Hold that line! Hold that line! Defense, defense!" And they go crazy every time one of their players makes a tackle or a touchdown. "We're number one! We're number one!"

Even a bad football team can rally from behind with the right cheerleaders, because praise is a powerful motivator. In fact, I've seen praise turn a mediocre player into a great one. There's something about praise that brings out the best in every one of us.

But what do you think would happen if a cheerleader suddenly turned negative? What if one of them laid down her pom-poms and started nagging? "Is that the best you can do? You guys are a bunch of sissies! My little sister could have made that tackle! Why don't you just go sit on the bench and give me the ball? I'll show you how it's done!"

That's a sight you've never seen, and you likely never will. If there's one thing cheerleaders understand, it's how to keep their guys motivated. Cheerleaders are an integral part of the game, and coaches know what a difference they make in how their players perform.

There's nothing more attractive to a guy than a woman who cheers him on, even when things are going badly. That's just as true in life as it is on the football field. If you want to know the key to a man's heart, it isn't food or money or even sex. It's praise. Men respond to praise. And wives who admire their husbands, cheering them on in both good and bad times, will always be attractive to them.

The Ephesians 5 model also gives men the key to staying infinitely desirable to their wives. What woman can resist a man who lays down his life for her, who loves her with abandon and cherishes the ground she walks on, and who throws himself into the job of meeting her every need?

In my marriage seminars, I often encourage each man to see himself as a gardener whose job it is to nurture and care for his wife. A good gardener knows what all the plants in the garden need, and he sees that they get it. He makes it his job to study each plant, to constantly watch and learn to help it grow strong and healthy. He learns just how much shade and sun and water and fertilizer each plant requires and how to work the soil for the best results. When weeds start to grow, he pulls them out. When flowers start to wilt, he prunes and transplants them. When cold weather sets in, he covers and protects the garden. A gardener does whatever he needs to do to see his garden grow lush and vibrant. He takes pride in his work because he knows that a healthy garden is the sign of a good gardener.

The same is true in marriage. A good husband is willing to do whatever it takes to see his wife grow strong and vibrant and happy.

He takes time to learn her needs and desires. He nurtures and shelters and protects. He provides for her physically, spiritually, and emotionally. He gives her all the love and attention it takes to see her blossom into the beautiful, exciting woman of his dreams.

2. It Releases the Potential in Our Spouse

A husband's primary responsibility in a marriage is to help bring his wife to her full potential before God. The Ephesians 5 model is designed to do exactly that. When a woman feels loved and protected and valued by her husband, it brings out the very best in her. It not only meets her most basic needs but also tempers any insecurities she might have. It gives her confidence and freedom to be the person God created her to be.

When Karen and I first married, I loved the way she looked at me. As a young bride, she looked at me with such love and admiration. I thought I was the greatest thing since buttered bread. But within a few years, all that changed dramatically. I found myself hating the way she looked at me. She had this hostile scowl, and several times in the middle of an argument I would call attention to it. "Stop looking at me that way," I would tell her. "I hate the way you look at me." It never occurred to me at the time that she was simply reflecting my own character and arrogance.

I was an enormous chauvinist at the time and treated her with contempt and disdain. I was an emotional bully and had all but destroyed her self-esteem. What I saw in her face was nothing more than a reflection of my own ungodly behavior and disposition.

But after God reached in and turned our marriage around, her facial expressions toward me started to change. I started learning the Ephesians 5 model and doing my best to try to live it out. The more I worked at it, the better I became at treating Karen with love and self-sacrifice. I began looking for ways to nurture and compliment her, and I started treating her the way God intended. And along the way a transformation occurred. Her face started to glow, and she became the beautiful woman I remembered marrying.

Today, nearly forty years later, Karen is more beautiful to me than the first time I saw her. I love looking at her, and I love the way she looks at me. And her self-esteem has never been greater.

I've watched Karen blossom from a shy, timid young girl who used to stand behind me at parties so that no one would notice her, to a powerful, influential television personality. She sits next to me during the taping of our weekly television show and radiates insight and authority. Her voice is still quiet, but her demeanor exudes confidence and wisdom. People have a hard time believing that she was once shy and timid.

Karen has become the woman of poise and influence that God created her to be. And I couldn't be more proud of her, because I know that she is reflecting the glory that I committed so many years ago to sowing into her life.

In the same way, Karen is proud when she sees the man that I have become and what God has accomplished in my life. She has watched me grow from an arrogant, long-haired, cigarette-smoking brute into an effective voice for the kingdom. Neither of us ever imagined the great things God had planned for my life and ministry, but he has used me in powerful ways to spread his message of hope and transformation. It's a daunting and humbling feeling. And Karen has played a huge role in helping me grow. She believed in me, even when I had lost all confidence in my own abilities. She has been there beside me every step of the way, building me up, cheering me on, telling me how great I am, whispering words of encouragement. Karen has been my faithful cheerleader, and because of that I've been motivated to accomplish far more in my life than I ever dreamed I would.

Men thrive in an atmosphere of praise and admiration.

Women thrive in an atmosphere of love and security and nurture.

3. It Disables Our Sin Nature

Sin is the ultimate destroyer of relationships. It seeps into a marriage and begins diluting and demolishing the bond that God created. Sin makes people do stupid and irresponsible things, it distracts us from our purpose, and it causes untold chaos and damage to families. But living out the Ephesians 5 model for marriage keeps sin at bay and disables our basic sin natures.

When Adam and Eve sinned in the Garden of Eden, their sins were not the same. The way they sinned actually reveals to us the differing sin natures of men and women.

In the garden, Satan came to Eve in the form of a serpent and began to tempt her. God had told Adam and Eve that they could eat of any tree in the garden except for one—the tree of the knowledge of good and evil. Eve knew that this particular tree was off-limits, but something inside her was curious. Somehow Satan sensed that, so he began to tempt and entice her with lies.

The serpent told her, "God knows that when you eat from it your eyes will be opened, and you will be like God, knowing good and evil" (Gen. 3:4). Eve chose to disobey God and eat the fruit. Then she convinced Adam to do the same.

When Eve was being tempted, Adam was right there in the garden, maybe even right beside her, yet she never took the time to consult him or ask his opinion. She also didn't wait to ask God about it, even though she knew she would be walking with God in the garden in the cool of the evening, as they did each day. Eve took it on herself to make a monumental, life-altering decision—one that she knew would forever change her relationship with both Adam and God. Yet she willfully chose to disregard God's mandate and eat the fruit.

Eve's sin was the sin of prideful independence. She wanted to be in charge. She wanted to know as much as God and be smarter than Adam. She looked at the fruit, looked at the serpent, and said to herself, *I am woman, hear me roar.* Then she took a big bite, completely disregarding the consequences of her decision.

And that dynamic is still alive today. The basic sin nature of women is to usurp authority, to take the reins and put themselves in charge—even when they know it's wrong—and to go their own way and make decisions that are not theirs to make. The sin nature of women is a bent toward prideful independence. It got Eve in trouble in the garden, and it gets families in trouble today.

Women are designed to be helpers to their husbands, equal partners within their marriages, and powerful voices of influence in every decision. They are gifted with a sense of intuition and reasoning that most men don't have, and they usually bring a unique point of view when it comes to making important decisions in the home. But when women ignore the counsel of their husbands and God and instead usurp authority, it creates chaos and friction. And it emasculates their husbands in the process. When women attempt to dominate their husbands, it flies in the face of what God intended for a healthy marriage.

So what is the sin nature of men?

In the garden, Adam was likely standing right beside Eve as she decided to willfully disobey God. Yet he didn't step in to stop her. More than that, he submissively ate the fruit when she offered it to him. He also did nothing to stop the serpent from tempting her.

Adam had been charged with the task of naming and subduing every animal in the garden, so when the serpent started questioning God's mandate, it was Adam's job to step in to put an end to the discussion. But he didn't.

Adam's sin was the sin of passivity. He chose to relinquish his responsibility and meekly stand by, even when he saw trouble brewing. He knew God had put him in charge, yet he refused to assert his God-given authority.

God has charged men to be leaders in the home, to provide and protect and initiate. Men have been given the task of guiding the family, of administering the affairs of the home, of overseeing their financial security, of shepherding their kids, of nurturing and cherishing their wives. Not dominating the family but steering its members toward holiness and godly living. Too often men choose to relinquish their role and stand idly by as women take the reins. They refuse to embrace their position of leadership and instead hand the torch to their wives.

I've seen many couples in my office who have allowed this kind of role reversal in their homes, and it always creates trouble. The wives almost always say the same thing: "If he would just take charge, I'd love to relax and let him lead. But he won't. And somebody has to be in control."

The sin of man is to passively abdicate his responsibility and let others take charge. The sin of woman is prideful independence—to desire authority and make decisions that are not hers to make. And these two sin natures feed off each other. They enable each other. They are codependent sins.

The Ephesians 5 model is designed to disable these sin natures.

When men begin to truly embrace their God-given roles of nurturing their wives, of providing and protecting and sacrificing, of leading and guiding, of shepherding and cultivating their families, of being the godly men that God expects of them, women are no longer tempted to try to usurp that authority.

When women truly embrace their God-given roles of encouraging their husbands, of respecting and honoring their authority, of praising and admiring them, of expecting the best from them, men are no longer tempted to passively relinquish their roles as husbands. They feel empowered to lead and begin to embrace the gifts and talents God gave them. They become the men God intended them to be, in part because they have a cheerleader who cheers them on to greatness.

Your Dream Marriage

The Ephesians 5 model is God's perfect plan for marriage because it is the only way for marriage to truly work. God designed us to live in harmony together, to complement each other, to be in perfect sync physically, emotionally, and spiritually. Not to be free of conflict, because conflict can actually be a healthy thing, but to have all the tools we need to work through conflict and make decisions together that are wise and intuitive and godly.

God designed husbands and wives to complete each other, not to compete with each other. Within the Ephesians 5 model, we find the key to that balance. A key that unlocks the door to the most rewarding, infinitely satisfying, lifelong love affair of our dreams.

10

Your Husband's Dream Wife

A good wife is heaven's last, best gift to man.

Jeremy Taylor

Two are better than one. . . . If two lie down together, they will keep warm. But how can one keep
warm alone?

Ecclesiastes 4:9, 11

Whenever couples book an appointment with me for marriage counseling, I usually make a couple of assumptions. I'm almost always right.

First, I assume that they're having problems in their marriage. This is a pretty easy bet, since they probably wouldn't be coming unless they were having serious trouble working things out on their own.

Second, I assume that it's the wife who suggested counseling. On this one I'm right about 95 percent of the time. It's almost always women who realize when it's time to see a counselor. Usually they have to drag their husbands—sometimes kicking and screaming—with them. Most men would rather spend an hour staring directly into the sun than talking about their marriage problems with a counselor.

That truth is evident in the first meeting. While the women are eager to talk about their problems, the men keep looking at their watch or staring at the wall with their eyes glazed over. It's obvious that they don't want to be there. But the fact that they are tells me they've tried everything else they can think of. Counseling is usually the last resort for a couple on the brink of divorce, but it shouldn't be. It should be our first response when we see signs of trouble in our marriages.

What Men Want

Women are usually the first to initiate counseling, but that doesn't mean they always like what I have to say.

I was recently counseling a couple when the husband started sharing his unmet needs. He had been quiet through much of the session, but suddenly he started opening up about all the ways he felt deprived and ignored. He talked about his need for trust and approval from his wife and how unappreciated he felt. He talked about the many times he desired intimacy but instead got a cold shoulder and an empty bed. He talked about his desire to do fun things together and his frustration that she showed no interest in his hobbies or plans for recreation. I was actually excited to see him finally open up and share his innermost feelings with his wife.

But all the while, she sat stone-faced and aloof. She barely responded, and when she did, she always downplayed his feelings. At one point the man turned in his chair to face his wife and said in frustration, "But these are my needs."

She slumped in her chair, let out a long, slow sigh, and said, "It just stresses me out when you talk about your needs."

It was an enlightening moment for me. As a counselor, I suddenly saw a huge key to the dysfunction in their marriage.

I got her attention, looked her square in the eyes, and asked, "Do you understand the concept of marriage? Do you understand that it's your job to meet his needs? If he could meet his own needs, then why would he have married you?"

I could tell by her response that she had never really thought of that before.

Her response wasn't that surprising. I see it a lot in my practice, especially among couples who are struggling in their marriages. A woman tends to downplay or misunderstand her husband's basic needs because they are so different from her own. But learning and meeting each other's needs is a critical step toward growing a healthy relationship.

If you lined up a hundred men in a room and asked them one at a time to tell you what they most need and desire from their wives, two surprising dynamics would appear.

First, every one of them would be able to answer that question. Most wouldn't even have to think about it first.

Second, their answers would be surprisingly similar. Though you would see some variation in how they phrased their needs or the degree of importance they placed on each one, most of the needs mentioned would show an amazingly consistent pattern.

Most men have four basic needs that they want met by a marriage partner:

1. They need to feel honored and respected by their wives.
2. They need sexual intimacy.
3. They need friendship—a wife who enjoys doing fun things together.
4. They need domestic support—a wife who takes care of the home.

Men are different in many ways, but when it comes to their basic marital needs and desires, all of them are very much alike.

Your Husband's Greatest Need: *Respect*

In my years of counseling, I've found that the single greatest need of every married man is *respect*. It's impossible for him to feel truly happy in a marriage if he doesn't get it.

This is not some unique discovery that I've stumbled onto. In fact, it's a truth that's been documented by nearly every serious study conducted on the dynamics of marriage. It's a universal truth that any marriage expert worth their salt understands, whether they're Christian or secular.

No woman will ever succeed in a relationship with a man until she learns to respect him. This is a rule with no exceptions. No loopholes. No escape clauses. No ifs, ands, or buts. Men are physically and emotionally incapable of binding their hearts to women who treat them with contempt and condescension.

Men gravitate to the place where they get the most respect, and they run from places where they feel disrespected. Men are terrified of dishonor.

A nagging, belittling wife will never get her husband to open his heart and let her in. But a wife who looks up to her husband, who gives him honor and praise, who exudes a gentle and quiet spirit toward him, will always have his full heart.

Many years ago, when Karen and I had been married only a couple of years, we had a terrible time getting along. We were both young and immature, and Karen would often belittle me. I hated the way she talked to me, but I couldn't blame her for it, because I was an emotional bully. Neither of us was happy in the marriage, and our speech toward each other reflected that truth.

One evening I was sitting in the living room watching a football game when an interesting thing happened—something I'll never forget. Karen was fixing dinner, and she brought a plate of food in for me. She bent over to place it on my lap, kissed me on the cheek, and gently said, "I love you." Then she smiled and walked back into the kitchen.

I didn't even respond, because I was in shock. I wasn't used to hearing her talk to me so nicely, because I never did anything to deserve it. I'm still not sure what got into her, but it had a profound impact on me. For the rest of the evening I couldn't even concentrate on the game. I felt a deep sense of conviction in my spirit. All the hateful things I had said to her kept coming to the surface of my mind, and I felt terrible. Her gentle act of honor and humility was like heaping burning coals on my guilty conscience.

That day I experienced firsthand the power of a gentle and quiet spirit. It was a lesson I've never forgotten.

When men feel honored and admired at home, they look forward to being there. They don't feel tempted to stay late after work or hang out with friends in the evening. They'd rather be home where they get the most praise.

Even more important, men who feel honored by their wives are far more likely to succeed at what they do. Praise is an empowering drug, and it has a way of propelling men on to greatness.

Years ago I heard a story about the mayor of a major United States city who spoke at a parade. Afterward he and his wife were strolling along the street hand in hand, and they passed by one of the many street sweepers cleaning up piles of trash and confetti left in the wake of the parade. The wife recognized the street sweeper as one of her old high school boyfriends. The three had a short conversation before the mayor and his wife continued on their way.

Halfway down the street the mayor leaned over to his wife and whispered, "Just think, if you had married him, today you'd be the wife of a street sweeper."

His wife smiled and whispered back, "No, if I had married him, today he'd be the mayor."

I'm not sure the story is true (most likely not), but it definitely could be, because a woman has enormous influence over her husband's future. When a woman believes in her husband—when she becomes his number one fan and cheerleader—it releases him to begin believing in himself. And men who believe in themselves almost always live up to their wives' expectations.

Your Husband's Second Need: *Sex*

Eighty percent of married men are more sexually oriented than their wives. They crave sex more often and desire more variety in their sex lives. Men are visually stimulated and are easily turned on.

Women, on the other hand, are more likely to want nonsexual affection. They want to cuddle and talk, but they often have much less desire for the act of sex than their husbands.

What this means is when it comes to sexual appetite, most men and women are completely out of sync. Not only are they not on the same page, they're not even reading from the same book. Almost all husbands want their wives to be more sexual, while many wives wonder how they ended up marrying the one man on the planet who seems obsessed with sex.

It's a dynamic that causes a tremendous amount of friction in marriages, especially among young married couples. Studies show that men reach their sexual peak at age twenty, while women don't reach their sexual peak until age forty. And even at their sexual peak, most women are far less sexually charged than their husbands. Because of this dynamic, most married couples are wired for conflict in the area of intimacy.

That's why a servant spirit is so critical to the success of a marriage. And nowhere is that spirit needed more than in the area of sex.

Paul addressed the topic of sexual intimacy in his first letter to the Corinthian church.

> But since sexual immorality is occurring, each man should have sexual relations with his own wife, and each woman with her own husband. The husband should fulfill his marital duty to his wife, and likewise the wife to her husband. The wife does not have authority over her own body but yields it to her husband. In the same way, the husband does not have authority over his own body but yields it to his wife. Do not deprive each other except perhaps by mutual consent and for a time, so that you may devote yourselves to prayer. Then come together again so that Satan will not tempt you because of your lack of self-control.
>
> 1 Corinthians 7:2–5

Paul understood that unmet needs within the covenant of marriage are a profoundly dangerous thing. When men and women don't meet their partner's needs, it gives Satan a powerful foothold for temptation. This is true with all marital needs but especially when it comes to sexual intimacy.

Men have a deep physical and emotional need for sex. And women have been given the gift of sex. When women choose to withhold that gift from their husbands, it creates a breeding ground for sexual sin and temptation.

Men don't just desire sex from their wives. They need it to feel fully whole and complete as marriage partners.

When we enter into the covenant of marriage, we actually surrender the rights to our own body to our partner. In Paul's words,

"The wife does not have authority over her own body but yields it to her husband. In the same way, the husband does not have authority over his own body but yields it to his wife."

Nowhere in Scripture are we given a more graphic example of what it means to become one flesh. In marriage we willingly commit to granting our partners full and complete access to everything we have, including our bodies. It is the ultimate act of service and humility.

The advice I give married women who don't feel sexual toward their husbands is to basically "fake it till you make it." As strange as it may sound, I encourage them to start acting more sexually interested than they are—to learn what turns their husbands on and to become their temptress. I explain to them that sex is a gift they have—a gift that God has entrusted to them—and gifts are not something you put on the shelf to admire. You have to use and exchange them in order to have fun. I tell women to learn how to become more sexual than they feel because their husbands need that from them. Women who heed that advice almost always find tremendous joy and pleasure in sexual intimacy—far more than they ever expected.

Several years ago I received a letter from a woman that beautifully illustrates the power of a servant spirit within marriage. Her letter chronicled an extremely difficult season in their marriage. Her husband had gone through a three-year period of pain and turmoil. He had been betrayed by several of his co-workers and had suffered numerous setbacks in his career. Friends had also cheated and deceived him. In almost every area of life, he felt emotionally beaten and battered.

She wrote, "During this time our relationship became estranged and I became the enemy, along with almost every other person in his life. Nothing I did was acceptable to him. One day the Lord spoke to me very clearly and told me that the only open door to his spirit was through sex."

She went on to explain that her husband was not very appealing to her during this time because of his anger and resentment, but she was committed to obeying the Lord's voice and helping her husband heal. So she began opening up to him sexually. She pursued and wooed him in spite of his anger and depression. Even when he pushed her away, she continued to make him feel desirable. Little by little he began to open up to her. Soon their marriage, along with his wounded heart, started to heal.

"As a result," she wrote, "God did the miraculous in our lives. He has been faithful in our marriage to go beyond restoration. I can't adequately describe the strength of our relationship. It is simply amazing."

Imagine how difficult it must have been for this woman to pursue her husband as he began to withdraw from the relationship. She loved and accepted him, even in the midst of rejection. It took a tremendous amount of patience and humility. But she understood the difficult season her husband had been through and was committed to helping restore his battered sense of self-worth.

That's what it means to have a servant spirit. It means putting your own needs aside and instead focusing on the needs of your partner. It means giving, even when you don't receive back. It means loving, even in the face of indifference. The woman who understands this truth will forever be the wife of a happy man.

Your Husband's Third Need: *Friendship*

Friendship is where almost all marriage relationships begin, and friendship is the glue that keeps marriages from getting old and stale. While women tend to bond through meaningful conversation, men bond through having fun together.

Having fun is how men establish relationships with other men. They don't become buddies by simply conversing with each other. They go golfing or skiing together, they play football, they ride bikes, they go fishing or sailing, they share similar interests and activities. Men bond through fun and entertainment. That's how they long to bond with their wives as well.

Numerous surveys indicate that men in happy marriages are far more likely to call their wives their best friends. And that's the greatest compliment a man can give.

Fun and sex are the two things that keep marriage from becoming a business relationship. If you remove fun and sex from the marriage, all you have left is a living arrangement.

All men need a buddy in life. Wives who can fill that role will go a long way toward keeping their husbands happy.

I once heard the story of a couple who had a deeply troubled marriage. Their relationship was so strained that it had reached the point of crisis. They had so many problems that they didn't know where to begin to fix them. Then one day the wife had a revelation. She realized that if she didn't do something drastic, their marriage could be over. So she went to her husband and asked him to take her hunting with him. She knew that hunting was his favorite sport, and though she had never shown any interest in going with him, she was committed to doing whatever it took to heal their strained marriage.

Her husband wasn't sure what to think, but he couldn't think of a good reason to tell her no, so he reluctantly took her hunting with him the following weekend.

That hunting trip became the catalyst that literally saved their marriage. Though she had never had a desire to hunt, she quickly learned to enjoy it. And this shared interest led them to start doing other things together. They learned to become friends again, and it restored their relationship.

Men need fun to grow close to another person. When men are having fun, they become emotionally open and vulnerable. They talk about things they otherwise might keep to themselves. They begin sharing their hearts. Like soldiers in a foxhole, they feel a oneness with those around them, and that oneness turns into a strong sense of connection.

Many wives don't understand this dynamic. They see their husbands doing things that they have no interest in, and they shrug it off. They think, *He has his hobbies and I have mine*, and they never give it much of a second thought. But that's not how their husbands see it. What their husbands see is a wife who has no interest in drawing close to them.

When you say to a man, "I'm not interested in the things you do," what he hears is, "I'm not interested in you." That's a dangerous message to give in a marriage relationship.

Husbands and wives who have fun together—who have shared hobbies and activities, who enjoy doing the same things, who spend time laughing and playing together—will always share a bond that is not easily broken.

Your Husband's Fourth Need: *Domestic Support*

Many of us are old enough to remember the original family sitcoms from the fifties and sixties like *Leave It to Beaver* and *Father Knows Best*. That was when television was still wholesome and inoffensive.

Most of those shows had a common theme—the wives would stay home and take care of the house and kids while the husbands went off to work. The husband would come home in the evenings and be greeted at the door with a smile and a kiss. The wife would always be dressed in a frilly apron and pearls. She'd hand him his pipe and paper and then help him settle into his big easy chair before scurrying back into the kitchen to finish getting dinner on the table. Dad was "king of the castle," and Mom was there to make sure he was taken care of.

This was Hollywood's version of home life during that time. I grew up in the fifties, and I can honestly say that life wasn't quite that blissful. I don't remember any pipe and paper waiting for Dad when he got home, and I never once saw Mom wear pearls with her apron. By the time Dad walked in the door, she was usually so frazzled that she needed help taking care of the kids, so he'd roll up his sleeves and dive in.

But the basic idea of those shows was something most of us could relate to. In most families, Dad was the provider and Mom took care of the home. They had distinct roles to play in the family, and both understood those roles. Most of the families I grew up with lived on one income and money was often tight, but life seemed much simpler and less stressful. Overall, families seemed happier.

Anytime I talk about the differing roles of husbands and wives in the home, I risk offending the majority of women in the audience. Today more than half of all wives work outside the home, and many families couldn't get by otherwise. Times have changed, and I'm not trying to turn the clock back to the fifties. But I also know how men and women are wired, and some truths will never change.

Women, by nature, have the gift of nesting. They are happier and more content when they're focused on their homes and families. Not only that, but they're much better at it than men. Women are more domestically centered than men, and I believe that's because God created them that way.

In the book of Titus, older women in the church are commanded to "teach the young women to be sober, to love their husbands, to love their children, to be discreet, chaste, *keepers at home*, good, obedient to their own husbands, that the word of God be not blasphemed (Titus 2:4–5 KJV, italics mine).

The Greek word translated in this text as "keepers at home" is *oikourous*, and it's a word derived from two different Greek words. The first, *oikos*, means a "house" or "dwelling," and the second, *ouros*, refers to a "keeper" or "guardian." A more accurate translation of the word might be "housekeeper" or "one who watches over the home."

Titus was encouraging women to pass down the art of housekeeping and to train the younger women how to keep their homes running smoothly. God created women to be domestically centered and then encouraged them to embrace that role.

Women, by nature, are more nurturing than men. They are more visually oriented and enjoy surrounding themselves with pretty things. Most women enjoy decorating and adorning and beautifying their homes. Women are most fulfilled when they're creating an atmosphere of beauty and protection.

That's certainly true with Karen. She is an extremely talented and gifted person and is capable of excelling at any profession she might choose, but she prefers to use her talents at home, doing what she most loves to do—taking care of the home and family. She is far more gifted at that than I am. That's true for most other women as well.

And men are more content when their wives do that. They enjoy coming home to a warm and comfortable house, to kids who are fed and protected and nurtured, to a hot meal and a clean home. Men also feel more needed and empowered when they're providing for their families. It gives them a sense of accomplishment and fulfillment and purpose.

Roles may have changed, but reality hasn't. In spite of what you've heard from the modern-day "women's movement," women are still happier when they're taking care of the home. And men are happier when they feel taken care of. Men still desire a wife who enjoys nurturing the family and taking care of the home.

This doesn't mean husbands should get a free ride while wives do all the housework. No husband should expect his wife to carry that load alone. Men are expected to help and do their fair share around the house.

I don't have the gift of turning a house into a home like Karen does, but I do know how to help out. I partner with her when it comes to doing chores, and I look for ways to help. If I walk by the laundry room and see clothes in the dryer, I take them out and fold them. If I see dishes in the sink, I load the dishwasher. If the den needs vacuuming, I don't wait for Karen to do it. I grab the vacuum cleaner and start working. Karen is a marvelous housekeeper and she doesn't even need my help, but I help her just the same, because that's what servants do. They look for ways to serve.

Women, on the whole, are better at taking care of the home. They are gifted with the skills and talents needed to create a clean and comfortable atmosphere. And men thrive in a home that is clean and comfortable.

Women are wired to nurture, and men have a deep need to be nurtured. It's just that simple.

Godly Submission

When Scripture commands women to submit to their husbands, it isn't somehow diminishing their identities or downplaying their significance in the marriage. Men and women are equal in every way, and men have no right to control or dominate their wives. Submission is not about subservience; it's about humility and kindness. Godly submission is simply a decision for wives to lovingly respect their husbands as their partners in life and to work alongside them to guide their families and make decisions together.

Husbands are commanded to do the same thing. Men are told to lay down their lives for their wives and to serve them by sacrificially meeting their needs. Men are expected to love their wives and to respect their opinions—to listen to their ideas and work as a team in the decision-making process.

Marriage is a two-way street—two servants in love, each committing to do whatever it takes to meet the needs of the other. It is through godly submission that a woman finds the key to her husband's heart. And it's through unlocking her husband's heart that she finds the love and worth she most needs and desires.

Godly submission is one of the most misunderstood concepts in all of Scripture. Throughout the ages, men have used the term to subdue and dominate their wives. When I was a young married man, I would often throw my weight around by reminding Karen that it was her job to submit to me. But God's view of submission has nothing to do with control. It's about humility, gentleness, and purity of heart.

In his first letter, the apostle Peter gave some interesting advice to wives with unbelieving husbands, and in the process he gave us all a clear illustration of what godly submission looks like.

> Wives, in the same way submit yourselves to your own husbands so that, if any of them do not believe the word, they may be won over without words by the behavior of their wives, when they see the purity and reverence of your lives. Your beauty should not come from outward adornment, such as elaborate hairstyles and the wearing of gold jewelry or fine clothes. Rather, it should be that of your inner self, the unfading beauty of a gentle and quiet spirit, which is of great worth in God's sight.
>
> 1 Peter 3:1–4

In the passage, Peter is primarily addressing wives of unbelieving husbands. He commanded these women to treat their husbands with the same respect and submission that they would their believing husbands. He gave no distinction. Peter understood that it is only through honor and praise that a woman can hope to make a difference in her relationship with her husband. That's true regardless of her husband's beliefs or standing with the Lord.

But the passage also has another message. Peter redefined for us what godly submission looks like. Peter encouraged wives to win their husbands over "without words," but instead through "purity and reverence." He told them not to focus solely on outward beauty but instead to honor their husbands through their "inner self, the unfading beauty of a gentle and quiet spirit, which is of great worth in God's sight."

God responds to a gentle and quiet spirit because it is a sign of respect and honor and humility. This is what godly submission looks like. And husbands respond to those same qualities in a woman.

The Wife of Your Husband's Dreams

Wives who set out to fulfill their husbands' basic needs will usually do so, because the checklist isn't really that long. It takes work and effort, but most wives are willing to do what it takes to keep their husbands happy. If they're looking for a good marriage, then this is where they begin.

But most wives aren't content with having a *good* marriage. What they want is a *great* one.

A wife wants a husband who isn't just satisfied with the marriage but who is infinitely happy and fulfilled. She doesn't want to be just a good wife; she wants to be the wife of her husband's dreams! And that isn't accomplished by checking off a list. It's done by developing a true servant spirit, by looking past her husband's basic needs and discovering his most intimate longings and desires.

A husband needs to feel honored and respected by his wife. But what he *desires* is to be the only man in her world she looks to for leadership and protection. A woman whose heart belongs only to him.

A husband needs sexual intimacy. But what he truly *desires* is a woman who is completely satisfied in his arms. A woman who not only gives him sex but deeply desires him as a sexual partner.

A husband needs to do fun things with his wife. But what he *desires* is a true best friend. A woman who doesn't just share his hobbies and interests but who truly enjoys having fun with him.

A husband needs a wife who takes care of the home. But what he truly *desires* is a wife who finds her happiness and fulfillment in becoming his domestic center—in nurturing and protecting her family, in creating an atmosphere of love and warmth and comfort. A woman who knows how to take a house and make it a home.

You don't build a great marriage by simply doing what's expected. You build a great marriage by becoming what your partner most longs for in a mate.

11

Your Wife's Dream Husband

If you treat your wife like a thoroughbred, you'll never end up with a nag.

Zig Ziglar

[Man] is the image and glory of God; but woman is the glory of man.

1 Corinthians 11:7

A good friend of mine was once in bed next to his wife. It was late at night and the room was dark. This was during a time when everything seemed to be going his way, and he remembers thinking about how great his life was turning out. He was lying on his back with his hands folded behind his head.

He said to his wife, "You know, I've never been happier than I am at this moment."

He waited for a response, but none came. After a few seconds he felt the bed shift as she rolled onto her side. Then suddenly she started to cry. "What's the matter?" he asked. His question made her sob even deeper.

"I've never been this unhappy," she answered through tears.

Needless to say, it wasn't what he expected.

That simple conversation began an awakening in my friend that eventually transformed their relationship. He never knew how unhappy his wife had become, simply because he had never taken the time to ask.

Like most husbands, he had always assumed that if *he* was happy, *they* were happy. But that's not always the case. In fact, sometimes it's the exact opposite.

I often tell men, "You're not a successful husband until your wife says you are." I'm not sure all men appreciate hearing that. Some are even visibly insulted, but I stand by the statement. The only true barometer of a healthy marriage is a happy and secure wife. And the only sure way to know if she's happy and secure is to ask.

When husbands are reluctant to do that, it's almost always because they're afraid of the answer they might get.

A Primal Wound

There is a deep wound inside the hearts of most women today. It's a wound that comes from thousands of years of neglect and abuse and disrespect at the hands of men. Throughout history, women have been seen as second-class citizens. During the time of Jesus, women were treated like cattle, and in many societies today, that's still the case. They are seen as property to be used and traded at will.

Even in this country, women have had to fight for their right to be heard. They had to fight for the right to vote and still today have to fight for equal pay in the workplace. Women in politics are viciously attacked and ridiculed far more than their male counterparts. And women are almost always depicted as being intellectually inferior.

In far too many ways, women have been treated with disdain and condescension. And all too often they've been left to fend for themselves.

When Jesus walked the earth, he continually fought for the rights of women. He engaged them in intellectual conversation, praised them for wanting to learn, invited them to follow him, even encouraged them to become disciples. These were scandalous acts in an age when women were considered invisible and powerless. Throughout the Gospels, we see Jesus challenging the deep-seated, patriarchal assumptions about women. He had a special place in his heart for those who were discounted by others, and women clearly fit into that category.

One of the great tragedies of our time is that men still tend to discount women—Christian men included. They discount women in the workplace, in churches, in the government, and even in their homes. Too often men have not cherished their wives enough to fight for them.

It is a man's responsibility before God to help bring his wife to her full potential. Paul tells us in 1 Corinthians 11:7 that man "is the image and glory of God; but woman is the glory of man."

So often I see women in my office who seem beaten down and depressed and insecure. Their self-esteem is at an all-time low, and their eyes seem sad and empty, like they have nothing left to give. They reflect no glory. All I see is pain and neglect and emotional abuse. When I look in their eyes, what I see is the reflection of a deeply hurtful and insecure husband.

The Measure of a Man

If you want to see the true character of a man, look at the countenance of his wife.

When you see a woman who is beaten down and vulnerable, you're seeing the reflection of a man who is severely wounded—and wounding. A man who refuses to embrace his responsibility before God.

In the same way, when you see a woman who exudes confidence and security, a woman whose eyes shine with glory, a woman of poise and beauty and self-assurance, you're seeing the reflection of a man who understands what it means to love and cherish his wife as Christ loves the church.

Jesus gave everything for us. He literally laid down his life to bring us into relationship with him. He held nothing back. And God commanded husbands to give everything for their wives. They are expected to lay down their lives to bring their wives to their full potential before God. A godly man holds nothing back when it comes to loving and nurturing his wife.

There will come a day when every man will stand before Jesus and give an account of his life. On that day, Jesus is going to look him in the eye and ask, "How did you treat the precious women I put in your life? How did you treat your wife and your daughters?"

Every man will have to answer that question. Thirty-eight years ago I would have bowed my head in shame, but thankfully, God reached in and changed my heart and life. Today I am deeply proud of the woman Karen has become. She radiates poise and confidence, and I'm honored to be her husband. I can look Jesus in the eye with full confidence and say, "You created her in her mother's womb to do great things on earth, and with your help, I have done all I could to help release that potential in her."

Men, you and I have been given an incredible responsibility. We have been entrusted with some of God's most prized and precious possessions—his beautiful daughters. How we respond to that responsibility has profound and eternal consequences in the eyes of God. It is a daunting and extraordinarily significant task that should not be taken lightly.

What Women Want

In Ephesians 5, Paul tells husbands to "love their wives as their own bodies" (v. 28). He goes on to write, "After all, no one ever hated their own body, but they feed and care for their body, just as Christ does the church" (v. 29).

I've always been intimately in tune with what my body needs. When my stomach rumbles, I make a beeline for the refrigerator. When my throat gets dry, I immediately get a tall glass of water. When my eyes get heavy, I know it's time for bed. When my feet hurt, I find a comfortable chair. When my pants won't button, I start cutting back on the burgers and might even suffer through a few salads at dinner. If that doesn't help, I start spending some time at the gym.

I know what my body needs and when my body needs it. I'm the only one who knows these things, so if I don't take care of them, no one else will. I've learned to watch for signs of hunger or fatigue or pain, and I tend to those needs when they come because I love my body and know it needs to last me a long time.

The same is true with you. When it comes to our bodies, we're all instinctively dialed in.

God expects us men to have that same level of care and intuitiveness when it comes to our wives. It's our job to train ourselves to love and nurture them, just as we do our own bodies—to learn how to recognize the warning signs of pain or neglect or discomfort and to tend to those needs as they come.

When we see signs of insecurity, it's our job to build up our wives. When we see signs of fear, it's our job to shelter and protect them. When we see signs of sadness, it's our job to bring them back to joy. When they cry, we comfort them. When they hurt, we salve and bandage them.

We love and nurture and cherish our wives, because if we don't do it, no one else will.

Just as a man needs a wife who will tend to his basic needs and desires, a woman needs a husband who cares about her needs and makes it his job to fulfill them. What she most needs from him can be summed up in four basic categories:

1. Women need security. They need to know that their most basic needs are taken care of, that they are secure physically, emotionally, and financially. They need to feel nurtured and cherished and loved.
2. Women need affection. They need nonsexual intimacy and care.
3. Women need communication. They need a husband who will open his heart and communicate honestly, without reserve.
4. Women need leadership. They need a husband who is willing to take charge and guide the family.

Your Wife's Greatest Need: *Security*

I was conducting a marriage seminar, and during one of the breaks a gruff-looking husband came up front to talk to me. I had seen him sitting alone near the front of the auditorium, and he told me he and his wife were having serious problems in their marriage. I asked him if his wife had come with him to the seminar, and he said, "Yes, she's here. She's sitting way back there in the back row." He told me they'd had a fight before they left home and she was so angry that she wouldn't even sit with him during the seminar.

We talked for only a few minutes, but during that time he called his wife "goofy" about a dozen times. Each time he'd tell a story about her, he'd roll his eyes and call her goofy.

At one point I asked him, "Are you aware of how many times you've called your wife goofy?"

He threw his hands up and shrugged his shoulders. "Well, she *is* goofy!"

I asked him if he called her that in front of the kids, and he admitted that he did. "I probably shouldn't do that," he said, "but she just acts so goofy I can't help myself." He used the term as if it were some kind of pet name.

At one point he was telling me what a terrible marriage they had, how they had no level of intimacy, no sexual relations, and almost no positive feelings for each other. They were completely distant and disenfranchised from each other. Yet he seemed to have no clue why that was.

When he finished, I leaned forward and said to him, "You do realize that I'm on your wife's side, don't you?"

He leaned back and stiffened his neck as I continued. "Are you aware how disrespectful it is to your wife when you call her goofy? No wonder she doesn't want to have sex with you. No wonder she doesn't want to be intimate. You have completely invalidated her as a person."

In the few short minutes we had, I explained to him how wounding and hurtful his words had been and what constant criticism does to a marriage. I challenged him to completely change the way he related to his wife to begin healing their strained relationship.

That night when the two of them were getting ready for bed, he said to his wife in a joking voice, "Well, Jimmy Evans told me I had to apologize to you for calling you goofy, so I guess I need to say I'm sorry."

His wife didn't laugh. She just sat down next to him and began to cry. "Do you know how disrespectful that is to me?" she asked him. "Do you know how much it hurts when you do that?"

Her response wasn't what he expected, but it opened the door for her to share her heart with him in a way she hadn't been able to before. The two of them sat on the edge of the bed and talked late into the evening. It was the beginning of a healing process that literally transformed their marriage.

That night he promised he would change, and he made a commitment to do whatever it took to restore their marriage. He has remained true to that commitment, and today they are closer than they ever imagined they could be.

It's almost impossible for a woman to bind her heart to a man who discounts and belittles her. Just as a man needs to feel honored and respected by his wife to draw close, a woman needs to feel loved and cherished. She needs to feel secure in the relationship. She needs to know that she is valued, that what she says matters, that what she thinks and does and contributes to the marriage is recognized. She needs to know that her husband cares.

When Jesus came in and began to transform my heart and life, this is one lesson he had to work overtime to drill into my mind. I've always been an off-the-charts type A personality, so I seldom admit to being wrong. In my mind, opinions tend to become facts the minute I say them aloud. I'm often stubborn as a mule, strong as an ox, and right as rain. That's not a good combination when you're trying to build a happy marriage. It took a lot of retraining before I finally started treating Karen with the esteem and value she deserves.

Since that time, I've been amazed to discover just how bright and intuitive Karen really is. I never knew that about her when we first married. I just thought she was this gorgeous woman who adored me. I never thought to ask if she had a brain. I figured we needed only one mind between us, and I had that area sewed up. I've since discovered otherwise.

I'm a very logical thinker, and when I make my mind up on an issue, I'm pretty set on it. Most subjects are black and white when you look at them logically. But Karen has a way of seeing an issue from a different perspective, and often she will come to me in her gentle way and say, "I'm sure you're right, but have you thought of it this way?" Then she'll challenge my long-held assumptions.

I usually nod my head and tell her I'll think about it, but I'm still pretty convinced I'm right. Then over the next few weeks or months her challenge will start to gnaw at my brain. I'll lie awake at night thinking about it, chewing on it, dissecting it, contemplating it. Then one morning I'll wake up in a cold sweat and think, *Oh my goodness, Karen is right!*

It still drives me nuts when that happens. But it's taught me an invaluable lesson about cherishing Karen's gifts and contributions in our marriage. She is the brightest, most intuitive woman I know, and it's my job to make sure she knows that.

For a woman to feel loved and secure in a relationship, she needs to know how much she is valued. She needs to know that she is the most important person in her husband's world. She needs to feel that she is taken care of in every area of life.

As husbands, it's our job to make the sacrifices and commitments needed to help our wives feel that way. We need to learn to live within our means, set a budget, and hold ourselves to it. To save, invest, and prepare for the future. To draft a will, buy life insurance, and keep good records so that our family is protected. To live in a safe neighborhood and find a life-giving church to attend. To be willing to work two jobs if that's what it takes to keep the family financially safe. To take charge of the household chores, make needed repairs, and keep our cars serviced, our appliances working, and our lawns mowed.

And we need to be a strong rock of authority to our kids. To instigate family devotions and prayer times, to oversee our kids' spiritual training, to make sure they do their homework, to repel destructive and ungodly friends.

As husbands, it's our job to keep our families on track and running smoothly, because that's what wives need to feel truly secure and safe and valued.

Your Wife's Second Need: *Nonsexual Affection*

Years ago I heard about a fascinating study on the sexual habits of men. They discovered that when married men are exposed to just three hours of R-rated material, they begin to objectify their wives.

It's not a surprising outcome, since women are almost always oversexualized in movies, but it's a dangerous dynamic for marriages.

When a man objectifies a woman, he no longer sees her as a unique individual. She becomes nothing more than a body—a means to fulfilling his sexual needs. And a woman knows when a man is seeing her that way. She knows when she is being looked at as one-dimensional.

When that happens in life, it's a sad thing. But when it happens in marriage, it's deeply destructive and degrading.

Women enjoy sexual intimacy with their husbands, but that can't be the only form of affection they get. If it is, the message is pretty resounding.

Women need nonsexual affection to feel loved and valued. They need to touch and cuddle to feel close. And they need words of affirmation to feel loved and appreciated.

Men are not really wired that way. When a wife curls up next to her husband, he instinctively thinks about sex. It's the first thought that pops into his mind. His normal reaction is to act on that thought. To him, that is showing affection. But his wife can easily get a different message. What she begins to think is, *I guess that's all I'm good for.*

Early in our marriage, I really struggled in this area. I grew up in a houseful of boys, and roughhousing was our daily way of relating. We were constantly wrestling and punching and putting each other in headlocks. It's how we connected with each other.

When Karen and I married, I showed her affection the same way. We'd be laughing and joking, and before long I'd have her in a headlock. She hated it and tried to tell me that, but I was slow to catch on. I actually remember saying to her, "You like this, you just don't know it yet."

It was honestly beyond my comprehension that she didn't enjoy roughhousing. I saw it as my job to enlighten her on how much fun it was.

I also had no idea how to be affectionate. Every time she touched me, I saw it as a sexual advance. In bed, all she had to do was breathe the wrong direction and I was ready to go at it. To me, sex was the ultimate act of affection, and I assumed that was true for Karen. But she didn't see it that way.

When God began transforming my heart, this was one area he targeted with a vengeance. I knew that Karen wanted me to change, but I really struggled with it. At one point I realized that in three years of marriage I had never once shown her affection that didn't lead to sex. Not once did I hold her or kiss her without wanting it to lead to the bedroom. God convicted my heart in a powerful way, and I committed to learning how to change. But it wasn't easy.

I remember praying so many times, "Lord, help me learn how to show affection to Karen." Those prayers were answered. Slowly I began to learn how to hold her and cuddle with her on the couch to enjoy being together. I found myself having to fight the urge to get up and lead her to the bedroom and instead just make myself sit and be gentle. It sounds strange now to admit, but at the time I honestly was deeply uncomfortable with the idea of hugging simply for the sake of hugging.

Before long I actually learned to enjoy it. Finally we could sit together and hold hands without it having to lead somewhere. And Karen was in heaven!

That's when an interesting dynamic began to unfold. The more nonsexual affection I gave Karen, the more sexually charged she became. Suddenly Karen became the aggressor, which was completely foreign to me. But I won't lie and say I didn't enjoy it. Quite honestly, I'm a little embarrassed by how easy I turned out to be!

A husband who understands the importance of gentle, nonsexual affection in a marriage will quickly learn the way to his wife's heart. Women need affection and touch to truly connect, and emotional connection is what turns a good marriage into a great one.

Your Wife's Third Need: *Open and Honest Communication*

Meaningful communication has the same effect on a woman that sex has on a man. She needs it to feel secure and satisfied.

When a husband talks to his wife, she is fully engaged in the conversation. And when the discussion becomes deep and intimate and meaningful, it's as fulfilling for her as sex is for him.

Some men may think I'm overexaggerating the correlation, but women know exactly what I'm talking about. Communication is a deeply personal and significant experience to women, and they need it to feel truly fulfilled in a marriage.

When I talk to women about their husbands' need for sex, I try to explain how critical it is to their sense of self-worth and satisfaction.

It is through the act of sex that men become one with their wives physically and emotionally. When they are deprived of sex, it begins to build a wall between them, and the longer they are deprived, the higher that wall becomes.

That same dynamic happens when women are deprived of meaningful conversation. They start to feel distant and disenfranchised. As time goes by, the wall between them and their husbands starts to grow.

When men are deprived of sex, the door to temptation is left wide open. That doesn't justify sexual sin in any way, because men are commanded to remain pure regardless of the struggles they feel at home. But it's naïve to ignore the reality that men are far more vulnerable to straying when their needs go unmet. The more deprived they feel, the greater chance they have of falling to temptation.

The same is true when women are deprived of meaningful conversation. They find themselves looking outside the marriage for an outlet. They begin craving and desiring intimate connection. Most women turn to their friends, but they soon find that it's not the same thing. The kind of closeness they crave can be filled only by a man, and they want that man to be their husband. When he doesn't meet that need, the door to temptation starts to open.

That's how affairs often begin. Men usually fall to sexual temptation, while women tend to stray through intimate conversation.

I give the same advice to men who don't feel very communicative as I do to women who don't feel sexual toward their husbands: "Fake it till you make it." To men who say that they are simply the strong, silent type and don't like to waste time talking, I tell them it is their responsibility as a husband to learn how to communicate with their wives, to teach themselves how to open up and share their heart and soul, and to learn how to engage in deep and meaningful conversation, even if it feels uncomfortable to them.

When couples are dating, men do this instinctively. Almost all men know that conversation is how you win a woman's heart, so they spend hours opening up and sharing their hearts. Then when they catch their prize, they get lazy and pretend they've completely forgotten how to talk. I don't buy it for a minute, and neither should their wives.

Women *need* communication. It's more than a desire to them; it's a need—a basic tenet of their survival as a wife and partner. And they need communication not just on a surface level. When women talk, they want to know details. They don't want to hear simply that you had a strange dream; they want to discuss every aspect of it. They want to hear the minute details of the dream, then talk about what each detail means.

When you tell them about your day, they need to hear specifics. Not just what you did at work but how you *felt* about what you did. Women long to hear about your innermost feelings. They need to hear about your hurts, your desires, your fears, your frustrations, your deepest longings. They want to connect heart to heart, soul to soul, spirit to spirit. It's our job as husbands to teach ourselves how to do that.

Just as a woman pleasures a man through sex by learning what he enjoys, a man needs to learn what pleases his wife during conversation. He needs to communicate on her level, not his own.

Men, this is a deep and abiding need that your wife has. If you want to get inside her heart, you do it through meeting that need.

Your Wife's Fourth Need: *Leadership*

One of the most common complaints I hear from husbands in my counseling office is that their wives are domineering and bossy. One of the most common complaints I hear from women is that their husbands won't take charge and lead the family. It's an interesting irony.

All over the country we have couples in a battle of wills. He's upset that she keeps telling him what to do, and she's upset that he won't take the initiative and do something. It would be funny if it weren't so damaging and destructive to marriages.

Just as every business needs a CEO, every home needs a leader. Someone to take charge and make sure that things stay on track. Someone to make sure the family is cared for in every way. Someone who understands the physical, spiritual, and emotional needs of every person in the home and takes responsibility for seeing that those needs get met.

God has charged husbands to fill that role. "The husband is the head of the wife as Christ is the head of the church" (Eph. 5:23).

God laid that responsibility squarely on the shoulders of men, and when men refuse to embrace that role, it is nothing short of a sin.

When men complain that their wives are too domineering, I tell them that leadership is like a big chair reserved for the CEO in the middle of the room. It's where people go when important decisions need to be made. When the kids have a problem they can't solve on their own, they go to the CEO for guidance. When someone has a question about friends or finances or school or other family dynamics, they consult the CEO. When issues of family vision or spiritual direction arise, everyone gathers around the CEO's chair to discuss it.

Every family has a chair of leadership, and someone has to sit there. Otherwise nothing gets done. The family can't function when the chair is empty. Wives instinctively understand that.

I tell husbands, "If your wife is sitting in that chair, it's because she's been waiting for you to sit there and you won't do it. But somebody has to be in charge."

All women long to have a man who will take initiative and lead the family. Even strong, independent women who are ambitious and forceful in other areas of life want a husband who will lift that burden from their shoulders at home. Women find their greatest security when they're with a decisive and confident man. That's a universal truth.

When a man embraces his role as the family's primary guide and shepherd, it creates an atmosphere of calm and safety. It eliminates confusion and chaos and instead builds a strong sense of emotional security and well-being. His wife is more content, his children are more secure, and the home runs much smoother. It is a model that works, because God set it up to work.

It's important to clarify, though, that leadership is not a license to dominate. Being in charge doesn't mean throwing your weight around or making unilateral decisions. It doesn't mean getting what you want when you want it. God didn't call men to be dictators; he entrusted them to be shepherds. There's a profound difference between the two.

Men and women are equal partners in the home, and they share equal say and responsibility when it comes to making decisions. Leading the home simply means initiating the well-being of the family and taking the primary role of guiding the family as you make important life choices.

Godly leadership is a daunting responsibility. It's not a right that comes from being born male, and it's not a position you use to get your way. It is a burden God places on your shoulders the minute you take on the role of husband. It is a position of sacrifice and submission—a decision to put your family's needs and desires ahead of your own.

I have spent over thirty years of my life pastoring a church in Amarillo, Texas, and they have been some of the most rewarding years of my life. But sometimes the responsibility feels overwhelming. I've spent many sleepless nights agonizing over important decisions that had to be made. I've spent hour upon hour in the prayer closet pleading for wisdom and guidance and clarity. As the senior pastor, I've had a lot on my table, and as the church has grown, my responsibilities have grown along with it.

I have the greatest staff a pastor could possibly want and the most loving, devoted congregation on the planet. I'm humbled that God has allowed me the privilege of leading such an unbelievable church. But the burden of shepherding such a large flock has often taken a huge toll on my heart and spirit.

Pastoring a church often looks like a glamorous calling, but only to those who haven't done it. Those who have can tell you what a formidable task it can be.

When I see a young leader preparing to pastor his first church, I'm excited for him, and I often give him words of encouragement. But in the back of my mind I'm thinking, *Son, I hope you're prayed up, because you have no idea what you're in for.*

The same holds true for men who take the reins and lead their families. Spiritual leadership is a daunting task, whether you're shepherding a church of ten thousand or a family of four. In both cases, leadership doesn't give you a license to control and dominate. It gives you an added weight of responsibility before God.

It's an overwhelming responsibility, but a deeply rewarding and humbling experience.

The Husband of Your Wife's Dreams

I recently heard the story of four young married men on their way back from a ski trip in Colorado. They all attended the same church and had recently completed a thirteen-week marriage course in their Young Marrieds class. The course was an intensive study on the basic needs of men and women in marriage, and these four young friends were discussing the class during their long drive home from the mountains.

They talked about how much the class had strengthened their marriages and what a great experience it had been. All four admitted to being surprised by how similar men were when it came to their basic marital needs. One by one they went over the four needs—respect, sex, friendship, and domestic support—and discussed why these needs were so important to them as husbands.

At one point there was a lull in the conversation, and one of the men asked, "So, what were the needs of women again?"

There was a long, awkward pause before one of them ventured a guess. "I think respect was one," he said, but they all agreed that wasn't right.

Finally one of them said, "I can't remember, but who cares? Let's talk about my needs again." They all laughed, but they were inwardly embarrassed that they honestly couldn't seem to remember.

Most guys tend to be pretty self-involved when it comes to marriage. We seem born with an intimate understanding of our own needs and desires, but we're often blind to the needs of those around us. When I first married Karen, I was convinced that she was there to meet my needs, but I never spent much time thinking about her needs and feelings.

Like my friend from the beginning of this chapter and these four young married men, I usually assumed that if *I* was okay, *we* were okay. But that's seldom the case.

Today I've learned that the only way to know for sure that Karen is happy and that I'm successfully meeting her needs is to ask. I make a regular habit of doing just that. I will sit down with her, look her in the eye, and ask, "How am I doing in our marriage? Am I meeting your needs? Am I meeting your desires? Is there anything you need me to do better?" Then I listen to her response.

I do this because only Karen knows if I am fulfilling my role as a godly and loving husband. And the only way I can know is to give her permission to tell me.

Men, I encourage you to do the same thing. Just because you are doing all you can to be a loving husband and father doesn't mean that your wife is happy and fulfilled. Take time to ask, "Do you feel satisfied in our relationship? Am I meeting your basic needs? Do you feel secure? Am I giving you the care and affection you need? Am I communicating with you the way you need me to? Am I leading and guiding the family the way God expects of me? Is there anything I'm doing in our relationship that you need me to do better?"

Ask, and then listen with a sincere heart and an open spirit. Don't be afraid of the answer. Just see this as your first step in becoming the husband your wife always dreamed of having.

Remember, you're not a successful husband until your wife says you are.

12

Two Servants in Agape

It is far more important to be the right kind of person than it is to marry the right kind of person.

Zig Ziglar

A happy marriage is the union of two good forgivers.

Ruth Bell Graham

My aunt and uncle had a wonderful, lifelong love affair. Their names were Peggy and Charles, and they had one of the strongest marriages I'd ever witnessed. They were a quiet, unassuming couple, and you'd never notice them in a crowd, but those who knew them best could tell you what an amazing couple they were.

When Uncle Charles died, I was asked to conduct his funeral, so I got a chance to sit down with Aunt Peggy and talk about the years they had spent together. As she was relating to me some of her special memories about my uncle Charles, she said something that both surprised and blessed me.

"Did you know that Charles wrote me a poem every day?" she said. "I didn't know that," I told her.

"Yes," she said. "He never missed a day in over forty years. Every morning he sat down and wrote a poem for me and left it on the dining room table before he went to work. They were such sweet poems. I loved reading them."

I'll never forget the sparkle in her eyes as she told me that. It was a side of my uncle I had never seen before. He was a strong, confident guy—a real man's man. I never took him for a poet.

Suddenly I began to see why their love for each other was so strong and vibrant and long-lasting. In that tender moment, I got a brief glimpse inside the heart of a man who truly understood what it meant to love and cherish a woman. I've spent years of my life encouraging men to cultivate an atmosphere of romance in their homes, but I've never seen a more shining example of what that looks like.

Aunt Peggy never had to ask her husband for a poem. It wasn't a condition of their marriage or something she expected from him. It was simply a gift that he could give her to make her feel special, so he took it on himself to do that for her. He wasn't looking for praise or rewards. He had no agenda or ulterior motives. He was simply a man who loved and treasured his wife, so he looked for ways to make her happy.

And that's what it means to have a servant spirit. It means going beyond what's expected and instead doing the unexpected. It means serving even when you don't feel like it. It means looking for unmet needs and then doing whatever it takes to fulfill those needs. More than that, it means going beyond meeting your spouse's needs and instead satisfying their inmost dreams and desires.

Anytime you see a great marriage, what you're looking at is two servants in love. You're seeing two people who have committed to putting their mate's needs ahead of their own. And when you see that, you're witnessing firsthand the true power of an Ephesians 5 marriage.

Five Levels of Fulfillment

In my years as a counselor, I've discovered that almost all marriages function on one of five different levels of happiness and contentment.

Though no two marriages are alike, all of them fall somewhere along this scale when it comes to marital fulfillment. These five categories are:

1. **Unmet Needs.** This first category is the worst. It's where two people are completely self-involved and show little interest in meeting each other's needs. These marriages almost always end up in the divorce court unless something drastic is done.
2. **Some Met Needs.** This second category is a little better but still frustrating. This is where couples meet a few of their partner's needs but are still rather selfish and oblivious to each other's feelings.
3. **Basic Needs Met.** This third category is where most Christian marriages seem to land. This is where couples are sensitive to each other's needs and usually make an attempt to meet them, but the demands and busyness of life often get in the way. They stay together and consider themselves relatively happy, at least most of the time, but there's always a feeling that things should be better. These couples usually say they have a "good marriage," but in the back of their minds, they know they aren't where they want to be.
4. **All Needs Met.** This fourth category is somewhat better. These are often the couples I see at my marriage seminars. They have good marriages but aren't quite content staying there. They find themselves seeking out the tools and skills they need to make their marriages stronger. They have a desire for more and are on their way to learning how to get to that point.
5. **All Needs and Desires Met.** This fifth category is the rarest. These are couples who have learned the secret to true marital happiness and fulfillment. And what they've discovered is that they get there by meeting not only their partner's basic needs but also their inmost desires. Like my uncle Charles, they aren't content with simply a *good* marriage; they want a *great* one. So they determine to go the extra mile.

This last category happens only in a marriage between two servant spirits. It happens when two selfless people are committed to putting the needs and desires of their mate ahead of their own.

They look for ways to build each other up, to love and honor, and to serve and sacrifice in order to help bring each other to their full potential before God.

Marriage Is a Skill

When couples come into my office for counseling, they always seem so tired and lost and frustrated, and they're usually embarrassed to be there. The first session is always the hardest on them because they feel so beaten down and defeated, like they've somehow failed at marriage and now have to go to the principal's office to see what they did wrong.

These precious people come to me because they know they need help, yet somewhere in the back of their minds they're afraid that I might judge them or look down on them. But nothing could be further from the truth. If anything, I admire them deeply for caring enough about their marriage to seek help. That's far more than I did when Karen and I were struggling in our marriage. It took me years to get to the point where I was willing to admit I was wrong.

I have a lot of respect for people who seek help for their marriages. They've tried to make it on their own but just can't seem to find the handles they need, so they humble themselves enough to seek guidance. They are good, decent people who want desperately to succeed; they just don't know how. This simple lack of knowledge is damaging their marriage.

When Karen and I found ourselves on the brink of divorce, it wasn't because we didn't care about each other. We wanted to have a good marriage. We wanted to feel in love again. We wanted to make our relationship work. We just had no idea how to do that. We were completely lost and bewildered.

Every couple needs certain tools and skills to build a happy marriage. We all are born with them; we just have to learn how to use them. We need to learn the proper techniques and methods, then form new habits and practices and develop new ways of thinking and responding.

Once we learn those things—once we understand what marriage is and what God expects from us as marriage partners, once we learn how to act and react to each other, once we start seeing our marriage the way God sees it—everything seems to naturally fall into place.

Defining Love

If you were to ask one hundred random couples if love was important to a happy marriage, every one of them would answer yes. But follow that up by asking, "How would you define love?" and you're likely to get a hundred different answers. We all know instinctively that love is the key to success in marriage, but when it comes to defining love, our views are all over the map.

No other word in the English language has been more twisted and perverted and misinterpreted than the word *love*. It's the most overused, overexploited, underappreciated, and misconstrued word in the dictionary. And not one definition we have does the word justice.

People say, "I love my wife." And in the very next sentence they say, "I love my car," "I love hot dogs," or "I love golf."

I love golf too, but how can I possibly compare golf to my wife? That's either a monumental insult or an unabashed compliment—depending on how I play on a given day, I suppose.

Women say to each other, "I love your hair like that." Men claim, "I love my team's new quarterback." Then we all go to church and sing, "I love you, Lord."

Am I the only one who thinks we should have different terms of endearment when describing hot dogs and God? We throw the word *love* around so much that it's completely lost any real meaning or value.

Those one hundred couples would be absolutely right: love is the key to growing a happy and successful marriage. But how in the world are we going to learn to love if we can't even define the word?

The original Greek language didn't have that problem. The New Testament was originally written in Greek, and it uses five different words when describing love and emotional attachment, whereas English has only one. These five words mean very different things.

When describing sexual feelings, the Greeks would use the term *eros*. Eros is a fleeting sentiment—more a state of being aroused than an emotional connection. When two eighteen-year-old kids say

"I love you" in the backseat of a station wagon, what they're really experiencing is *eros*.

When describing a family bond, the Greeks might use the term *storge*. This is the natural family bond you feel for relatives like brothers, sisters, or children. When you love someone like a brother, the term you're looking for is *storge*.

If you were to say, "I love my job," the Greeks would use the term *thumos*, or *epithumea*. It describes a strong, passionate feeling for something or someone. When you find yourself craving ice cream or cheering for your favorite sports team, what you're feeling is *epithumea*.

I have friends I really like, so when describing them, I might use the word *phileo*. It's a term of affection and endearment. The city of Philadelphia gets its name from two Greek words: *phileo* and *delphia*, which means "brother." When you combine the two, you get the phrase "city of brotherly love." When I hang out with my buddies from church, the feeling I have for them is *phileo*.

But there's a fifth word for love that is stronger and more intentional than any word we have in the English language. This word is *agape*, and it is perhaps the most powerful and unambiguous word in all of Scripture.

Webster's Dictionary defines the word *agape* as "selfless love of one person for another without sexual implications."[2] When I speak, I use a more exhaustive definition—one that I've compiled from several different sources. I describe *agape* as "a permanent, self-sacrificing commitment to act in the best interest of the other person regardless of negative emotions or difficult circumstances."

Agape is not a feeling or emotion. It isn't based on chemistry or affinity. It is a deep decision of the heart and will. It is a sacrificial love, an unwavering, unconditional, irrevocable love. And it is the only word in all of heaven and earth to adequately describe God's love for his people.

Agape Love

When John wrote, "For God so loved the world that he gave his one and only Son, that whoever believes in him shall not perish but have

2. *Webster's Online Dictionary*, s.v. "agape," www.websters-online-dictionary.org/definitions/Agape

eternal life" (John 3:16), the word he used was *agape*. Agape is the love God has for you and me.

When God says he loves you, what he is saying is, "I am making a permanent commitment to always do what's best for you, even when you disobey, even when you don't deserve it, even when you turn your back on me. I will never leave you, never forsake you, never give up on this relationship."

This is no fleeting feeling we're talking about. This is not a passing emotion or a simple term of affection. God's agape love for you is absolute and nonnegotiable. When John wrote, "For God so loved the world," he was saying that all the love in the universe is fully engaged in pursuing you, serving you, wooing you, cherishing you, and working to bring you into full relationship. God *loves* you, and that love is categorically unreserved. Resolute. Eternal.

God's love for you is the same yesterday, today, and tomorrow. It doesn't change with the seasons or grow weaker as time goes by. It doesn't falter when he's angry or diminish with age. He loves you because he decided to love you. It is a choice of his will. It is a resolution, not an emotion.

God is absolutely committed to this relationship, and he loves you in spite of your sins, in spite of your wayward heart, in spite of whether or not you deserve to be loved. If that doesn't bring you to your knees in humility before God, I honestly can't imagine what will.

And this is the kind of love husbands and wives are commanded to have for each other.

The Act of Love

Some Pharisees once came to Jesus and asked, "Which is the greatest commandment in the Law?" (Matt. 22:36). Jesus answered, "'Love the Lord your God with all your heart and with all your soul and with all your mind.' This is the first and greatest commandment" (vv. 37–38).

But he didn't stop there. Jesus went on to say, "And the second is like it: 'Love your neighbor as yourself'" (v. 40).

In both cases, the word he used was *agape*.

You and I are commanded to love the same way God loves. Not as a feeling or an emotion but as a decision.

I have very little control over my feelings, because feelings are fickle and fleeting. I may like someone today but be angry with them tomorrow. My emotions tend to rise and fall with the changing tide—one day high and the next low. But a decision isn't like that. Decisions are an act of the will. I can decide to love someone even when I don't like them very much.

Years ago I had a neighbor who was a really nice guy, and he would have been a perfect neighbor if it weren't for his demon-possessed dog. It barked at the most inappropriate times and often kept me up at night. It was one of the most annoying animals on the planet, and I had to live next door to it.

When people ask me if I think animals will be in heaven, I tell them I can't know for sure, but I believe they will, except for my neighbor's dog. It most definitely will not be there.

Because of that dog, there were days when I wasn't very happy with my neighbor. On those days I may not have liked him much, but that didn't keep me from loving him. I still wanted what was best for him, and I decided to do right by him, regardless of how I felt at a given moment. If he had asked to borrow my lawn mower, I'd gladly have obliged. If he needed a ride, I'd have given him one. I didn't have to feel kindly toward him to be kind to him. I had already decided to be kind and to love him as God expected me to.

God doesn't command us to feel loving, but to love. It is an action, not a reaction or an emotion.

When we act in love even when we don't feel loving, an interesting dynamic begins to take shape. Our feelings start to change as well. Our emotions tend to follow suit and we actually start to *feel* loving, even toward those who have slighted us.

Agape love says, "I choose to act in your best interest, regardless of how I feel at the time, regardless of how you act or react, regardless of what you deserve." Agape love is stable and constant and committed. It is the only kind of love that can withstand the inevitable trials and tribulations of life.

Deciding to Love

When couples come to me for counseling, there's a common phrase they almost always use. "We just don't love each other anymore," they tell me. They say it almost casually, with little or no emotion, as if they were saying, "I used to love guacamole until I ate a bad avocado, now I don't like it anymore."

All of these couples were once head-over-heels in love with each other. They had fallen in love and then stood at the altar declaring their love to God and the world, and they even promised to stay in love forever. But along the way they experienced pain and frustration and disappointment, and now they no longer felt the way they once did. They had fallen out of love as fast as they fell into it, and they'd come to me wondering how that happened.

I never judge these couples, because Karen and I once found ourselves right where they are—completely out of love. After just a few short years of marriage, we felt so beaten and battered that we had absolutely no feelings toward each other. We were completely and categorically "out of love." And we had no idea how to recapture the feelings we had lost.

Like the couples in my office, Karen and I had bought into a distorted and perverted view of love. When I said to Karen, "I love you," what I was saying was, "At this moment, I feel close to you. I'm attracted to you. You haven't offended me, so I have pleasant feelings toward you."

Our love was a dependent love. A conditional love. An *eros* love. Our love was a feeling, not a decision. And feelings are as fleeting and unpredictable as the weather. They can change not only day by day but minute by agonizing minute.

Only agape love is powerful enough to sustain a marriage. Only agape love can survive the inevitable struggles of two independent souls being molded into one flesh. Only agape love can bring a marriage to its full potential before God.

I'm so glad that God is not ruled by his emotions. I'm glad his love for us isn't based on his feelings toward us at any given moment. If it was, we would all be in serious trouble.

If I fell in and out of God's grace the way most couples fall in and out of love, I'd be well on my way to a horrible fate in eternity. You would too. But God's love isn't like that. He *chooses* to love, and because of it, you and I are accepted without condition, without fear, and without reserve, even when we don't deserve it.

Today I have that same commitment to Karen. I no longer base my love on her performance. I no longer gauge my love based on emotions or impulse. I have chosen to love Karen, regardless of the circumstances, regardless of how she looks or acts or reacts, regardless of the struggles that may come between us. I still remember the moment I made that decision over thirty years ago, and my resolve since that time has only grown stronger.

I love Karen. I *agape* Karen. Because of that, she has complete confidence in our relationship. There is absolutely no fear, no ambiguity, no uncertainty, no question in her mind that I will be there in the morning when she wakes up. Our marriage today is solid and secure and certifiably indestructible.

Karen and I *feel* deeply in love with each other, but much more than that, we have both made a conscious decision of the will to love each other. It is the decision, not the feeling, that keeps our marriage strong.

Three Attributes of Love

The apostle Paul wrote to the church at Corinth:

> Love is patient, love is kind. It does not envy, it does not boast, it is not proud. It does not dishonor others, it is not self-seeking, it is not easily angered, it keeps no record of wrongs. . . . It always protects, always trusts, always hopes, always perseveres. Love never fails.
>
> 1 Corinthians 13:4–5, 7–8

Whenever love is described in Scripture, it is always described as an action. It has attributes that are real and tangible and decisive. When you make a decision to love, Scripture gives all the concrete tools and resources you need to carry that out.

That's the beauty of a decision. It isn't left to chance or ambiguity. A decision is intentional and premeditated. It's like deciding to play football instead of soccer. Once the decision is made, you start gathering the equipment you need and then start practicing until you've developed the skills necessary to play. You keep practicing so that you can get better as time goes by. The better you play, the more you want to practice. The more you practice, the more satisfaction you get from the game.

Agape love is a decision, but it's also a skill, and skills need to be developed. Once you decide that agape love is what you want for your marriage, the next step is the commitment to practice. You start applying biblical principles to develop the skills you need to grow. The more you practice, the better you get. The better you get, the more satisfying your marriage becomes.

Agape love is a monumental concept with many different facets and dimensions. It's not a skill you develop in a weekend seminar. It's a journey of discovery and learning that begins with the first step and carries you to your final breath. Every day Karen and I learn new ways to serve each other, new ways to be kind, new ways to romance each other, new ways to show our commitment to love each other. Every day we get better at it. Love is a process that takes time.

In the next few chapters, we're going to dissect the concept of agape love even more. And we'll examine three of love's most defining characteristics.

First, agape love is *dynamic*. It is vibrant and active and growing. It doesn't rust with age or grow stale. Agape love is romantic and creative. It is a commitment to do whatever it takes to keep your relationship fresh and exciting.

Second, agape love is *fearless*. It is raw and naked yet without shame. It is rooted in certainty and free of doubt and insecurity. Agape love is perfect love, and perfect love casts out all fear.

Third, agape love is *covenantal*. It doesn't wane with time or diminish with age. It isn't based on performance or tied to emotion. Agape love is a covenantal love, and covenants are carved in stone.

Dynamic. Fearless. Covenantal. These three attributes of love can carry your relationship to greater heights than you ever imagined possible.

Let's take a closer look at these three critical attributes of love.

13

Dynamic Love

When I have learnt to love God better than my earthly dearest, I shall love my earthly dearest better than I do now.

C. S. Lewis

I will sing a new song to you.

Psalm 144:9

As a believer, I put a high priority on doing what's right. I hold myself to a high standard when it comes to living an upright and godly lifestyle. I try to do right by people and stay away from evil. I say my prayers, read my Bible, and do my best to set a good example for others. I shun even the appearance of impropriety to stay true to my calling, and I'm committed to staying the course, no matter how difficult the road becomes.

Christians are called to emulate Christ, and as believers, most of us work hard at doing just that. Striving to live in righteousness is a basic tenet of the Christian faith and an important standard for followers of Christ.

The trouble comes when we start to believe that that's what God most wants from us—that if we do what's right, avoid what's wrong, and keep our spiritual noses clean, we've achieved what God most desires of us.

But Scripture teaches otherwise. God looks at the heart, and a heart can easily grow cold, even when the head is fully engaged.

Perhaps the most chilling and sobering passage in all of Scripture for believers is found in the book of Revelation, when Jesus addresses the church at Ephesus. The passage starts out with a few words of encouragement:

> I know your deeds, your hard work and your perseverance. I know that you cannot tolerate wicked people, that you have tested those who claim to be apostles but are not, and have found them false. You have persevered and have endured hardships for my name, and have not grown weary.
>
> Revelation 2:2–3

Like you and me, the people at Ephesus were committed to living a righteous lifestyle. They worked hard at doing good and avoided evil at every opportunity. They stayed in the Scriptures to recognize right from wrong. They remained true to their convictions, even in the face of persecution. Ephesus was a good church filled with good and decent people.

But they forgot the most critical and fundamental principle of the Christian faith.

> Yet I hold this against you: You have forsaken the love you had at first. Consider how far you have fallen! Repent and do the things you did at first. If you do not repent, I will come to you and remove your lampstand from its place.
>
> verses 4–5

They forgot their first love. They allowed their hearts to grow cold and stale and lethargic. They neglected to fan the flame of their faith, and the passion had completely gone out of the relationship.

Their only sin was the sin of apathy, but that was all it took to fully snuff out the embers of their love.

When God Removes His Lampstand

God is a patient and forgiving God, and he has promised not to hold our sins against us. But he also refuses to take second place in our lives. Nothing is more insulting to God than when we push him off the mantel of our hearts. When God ceases to be first in our lives, it's only because another god has taken his place. That is something he never tolerates.

God loves us too much not to fight for our affection. He is a relentless pursuer of hearts.

Jesus warned the church at Ephesus that if they didn't repent and change their ways, he would remove their lampstand from its place. This is no small warning for a church that prided itself on being a godly house of worship.

When God places his lampstand in the midst of a church body, he is giving it his stamp of approval. It is his way of shining a bright light on the church, placing it as a glowing example to the world of what Christians are called to be. The lampstand is symbolic of God's divine anointing. It is like a beacon of light to an unbelieving world, drawing lost souls toward the radiance of God's love. Where the lampstand shines bright, the Holy Spirit shines even brighter.

When God removes his lampstand from a church, he is removing his blessing and approval. He removes the light to hide his people from a lost world. Lukewarm Christians are a bad advertisement for a passionate God, so he takes away his light to keep their indifference from infecting others.

Just as love is contagious, so is apathy.

The church at Ephesus wasn't always lukewarm. There was a time when their love for God burned hot and their passion ran high. They were a shining example of God's love, so he had placed a lampstand in their midst to show his approval. But somewhere along the way they got tired. They still practiced the art of "doing church," but their love for God took a backseat to the busyness of life. They kept their lawns mowed and their bills paid and even spent time in Scripture, but their desire for intimacy with God was all but forgotten.

Does that describe any marriage relationships you know? Do you know any couples who once burned hot with passion but now seem cold and distant and tired? Are you familiar with any marriages that are so mundane and lifeless and boring that they've long since lost their lampstand?

If you think a lukewarm church is a poor advertisement for God, imagine how he feels about a lukewarm marriage.

Losing Our First Love

A few years ago our MarriageToday ministry hosted a Caribbean cruise, and I took my mother along with us. My father had recently passed away, and I thought the fresh air and sunshine would lift her spirits.

One afternoon she and I were sitting on the deck next to a couple who looked to be in their fifties. The woman struck up a conversation with my mother and at one point asked her, "What does your son do for a living?"

My mother told her I was a pastor and that I also had a ministry to married couples. As soon as the words left her mouth, the man leaned forward in his chair, looked my mother in the eye, and shouted, "Marriage?"

Then the couple started laughing hysterically. My mother and I were in shock. We had no idea why they were laughing or what was so funny about my chosen career.

After a few minutes, the woman caught her breath and said to my mother, "I'm not his wife, I'm his girlfriend. He left his wife at home."

The man added to her comment by saying, "I paid a lot of money for this cruise, and my wife would have just ruined it for everyone, so I decided to bring my girlfriend instead. I wanted to have fun, not get into another fight."

The two of them continued to laugh about the irony of this meeting, but nothing about it seemed funny to me. All I could do was imagine his poor wife sitting home alone while her husband gallivanted around the world with his mistress. What a sad excuse for a husband. And what a pitiful advertisement for the beauty and sanctity of marriage.

I wasn't very amused by the man's comments, so I didn't spend much time talking to him. But I did find myself wondering what caused their marriage to become so numb and indifferent. I imagine that even this poor excuse for a couple was once two infatuated souls with a budding young romance between them. What happened to the love that had once burned so high? Why did they allow themselves to drift so far apart? When did they decide to simply give up and let their relationship die a slow and painful death?

When Flames Fade

We all start our married lives with passion and desire and a lust for even greater intimacy. We love doing things together and count the minutes when we're apart. We spend every waking moment thinking of new ways to show our love. Our hearts burn with attraction and our eyes sparkle with delight. Even in a crowded room, our zeal gets the best of us as we gaze longingly into each other's eyes as if we were the only ones there.

But somewhere along the way, something happens. Life happens. Our passion starts to fade. Our enthusiasm wanes and our hearts grow dim. We no longer jump for joy when our partner enters the room, and our times apart no longer feel so empty. Familiarity takes the place of romance, and we settle into a routine of coexistence. A relationship that once burned with desire now barely manages a spark.

It's a sad dynamic but not a surprising one. In fact, all relationships will naturally settle into a state of entropy when left unchecked and unguarded.

When God first saved me, I was on fire for the Lord. I couldn't stop talking about Jesus. I began sharing the gospel with all my friends, and I even scared strangers on the street with the wild look in my eyes. I couldn't imagine my love for Christ ever fading. But in time it did.

Like almost all believers, I soon found myself struggling to keep the flame alive. As my faith grew more familiar, my passion for God started to fade. Suddenly my first love no longer looked so lovely.

Today that's no longer the case. I can honestly say that I am more in love with Jesus than I was on the day he saved me. My passion for God is greater than it has ever been, but only because I have worked hard at keeping my love alive and my faith fresh. Years ago, when I realized that my heart was wandering, I began doing the things I needed to do to recapture the feelings I had lost. I was committed to the relationship, so I learned how to keep the relationship strong and vibrant and exciting.

As believers, we've all experienced lulls in our relationship with God. We've all felt our faith slipping into boredom. When that happens, we do what needs to be done to keep our hearts kindled and our faith vibrant. None of us wants to see God remove his lampstand from our lives, so we fan the flames of love and keep our passion alive.

That's why we go to church. That's why we seek out a Spirit-filled group of believers to worship with every Sunday and stay in the Word throughout the week. That's why we begin and end each day in prayer and then meditate on God at every opportunity. We've learned the spiritual disciplines it takes to keep our faith from dwindling, and we practice those disciplines to keep God first in our lives.

Don't our marriages deserve that same level of reverence and regard?

A Lampstand Marriage

I recently took time out of my schedule to learn how to fly a plane. It's one of those things I've always wanted to do but never made time for, so I finally decided to stop putting it off.

After completing all the requirements, it was finally time to take my final exam so I could get my license. My FAA instructor that day was a woman named Carol. She was quiet but nice. And I was scared to death. Not scared of flying but scared of Carol. I'm still not sure why, but somehow I felt like I was sixteen again, sitting next to a policeman in my old Oldsmobile, about to take my driver's test. I was a ball of nerves then, and I was a bigger ball of nerves sitting next to Carol.

She hardly said a word as I taxied the plane down the runway; she just kept writing on her pad and making notes. I wondered what awful things she was writing about me. *This can't be good,* I thought. *I've already flunked and I haven't even left the ground.*

We reached the end of the tarmac and were waiting for instructions from the tower when suddenly Carol asked me, "So what do you do for a living?"

"I'm a pastor," I told her. "And I also have a television ministry called *MarriageToday.*"

Carol didn't respond. She just looked down and started writing again. *Now I've done it,* I thought. *The one instructor on the planet who hates married men, and I have to draw her name!*

But then something interesting happened. Carol looked up at me, and I could almost make out a tear in the corner of her eye. She completely surprised me by saying, "You know, I married the perfect man. He is so good to me, even when I don't deserve it. He is truly a good man. He's an awesome husband, and I love him so much."

Carol's eyes lit up with excitement, and her voice lifted with pride as she told me stories of her wonderful husband. She told me how patient he was with her, even when she got angry. "I'm a Yankee," she said, "and I can be pretty stubborn. But he knows exactly how to stand up to me and defuse my anger."

She told me of the many times he'd surprised her with gifts and flowers for no particular reason other than to show his love. She talked about his faithfulness to her, his loyalty to the marriage, his kind and quiet demeanor. She told me how they met and how they came to marry. She couldn't stop praising her husband. Even during the flight exam, between drills and maneuvers, she would continue telling me stories about her husband.

This is a guy I'd really like to meet, I thought. *This is the kind of husband every married man needs to emulate.*

What a refreshing day that was. Not only did I pass my pilot's test, but I got the chance to meet a woman who exudes the kind of joy and satisfaction that every married woman should have. Their marriage was a powerful and glowing example of what a true servant-spirit marriage can be. I found myself thoroughly encouraged just being in her presence. Seeing Carol's face glow with pride made me want to be a more loving and caring husband. This was a marriage worthy of the brightest and tallest lampstand.

When I drove away from the airport that day, I couldn't wait to get home to Karen.

Hang on, baby, 'cause Hubby's about to get his romance on!

Remembering Our First Love

There's something about an exceptional marriage that makes us all want to be better husbands and wives. Seeing two people so deeply in love gives us a great sense of hope and expectation. We know that if they can do it, we can do it. Anyone can have a happy and successful marriage, and my unexpected conversation with Carol that day proved that fact.

What a sharp contrast that was to the depressing encounter I had on the deck of that cruise ship. Here in one corner was a man so selfish and self-involved that he could actually laugh about his adulterous affair while his wife sat home alone wondering where her husband was. In the other corner was a man so giving and caring and kind to his wife that she actually was fighting back tears as she described him to a stranger.

Which of those couples would you rather have over for Thanksgiving dinner?

Great marriages are not reserved for the fortunate few. Any couple can have a lasting, passionate love affair. It's not a matter of fate or luck or good genes; it's just a decision to do what you need to in order to get there.

Marriages don't die because of struggles or misfortune. Couples don't fall out of love due to familiarity or old age. Marriages fall apart when we forget our first love. Relationships lose their luster when we stop doing the things we did at first. When we stop courting each other, stop wooing each other, stop looking for the good in each other.

Marriages die when we allow them to atrophy. When we stop tending to needs. When we no longer work to meet our mate's deepest desires. When husbands stop watering the garden and wives leave their cheerleader outfits hidden in the back of the closet.

The key to reviving a struggling marriage is to go back to the beginning. To remember what it was that first brought you together and then begin reenacting your courtship. To start romancing each other again.

You remember your first love and then rekindle the flame by doing the things you did at first.

The Way We Were

In my drawer at home is a set of cuff links with my initials engraved on the top. I've had these cuff links for over forty-one years. Karen gave them to me on my seventeenth birthday. They're not very expensive, but they're worth more to me than all the gold in Fort Knox.

I met Karen when I was just sixteen, and I thought she was the most beautiful girl I'd ever laid eyes on. She was a stunning young woman with flowing blonde hair and a smile that would melt your heart right out of your chest. I couldn't believe she actually agreed to go out with me, much less start dating me.

Those cuff links were the first gift she ever gave me, and I've cherished them all these years. They mean more to me today than they did the day I got them, because they remind me of the many years we've been together.

As a teenager, I knew almost nothing about courting a girl. I lived in a houseful of boys, and our idea of a fun afternoon was playing full-contact football in the yard. Laying a good tackle on my older brother was as close to romance as I ever got. Especially if I was able to draw blood.

But all that changed the day I met Karen. I pulled out all the stops trying to impress her. I spent the first few months of our relationship studying everything she said and did. When she talked about things she liked to do or movies she wanted to see, I'd make detailed mental notes. And those are the things I planned for our dates.

I also paid close attention to things she didn't like, because the last thing I wanted to do was run her off.

At the time, I drove a 1964 Dynamic Eighty-Eight Oldsmobile. I loved that car, mostly because of the 394-cubic-inch, V8 engine. From the first moment I sat behind the wheel, I knew that I had finally found my purpose. I never realized what a "gifted" driver I was until I got my first car. I could take a corner faster than any kid in town, hands down. And I'm pretty sure that every cop in Potter County had my picture on their dashboard.

But I quickly learned that Karen didn't like fast drivers, so whenever I picked her up, I drove like a little angel. I'd use my blinkers and everything. I knew that if one of my buddies ever saw me, I'd lose my hard-earned reputation, but even that didn't faze me. I was on a quest to impress the prettiest girl in town, and that was all that mattered.

Karen often commented on what a safe driver I was, and I'd just smile and nod. She had no idea who she was talking to or how much restraint it took to keep my foot from punching the floorboard.

Rekindling the Flame

Isn't that how all love affairs begin? Don't we all have stories like that?

When we find our first love, we do everything in our power to impress them, woo them, court them, please them, draw them into our love. Their passions become our passions. Their hobbies become our hobbies. Their desires become our desires. We long to be with them, so we become people they enjoy being with. We learn how to romance them, even when we don't feel romantic.

But far too often we see romance as a way to begin a relationship, not a means of sustaining it. We allow our hearts to settle into a state of apathy.

I often compare stale relationships to a junkyard full of old cars. Every junkyard in the country is piled high with wrecked and rusty old automobiles—cars that are so beaten and battered that they no longer have a purpose. But every one of those cars started out on a showroom floor. They all began as bright, new automobiles, glowing with fresh paint and polished chrome, trimmed with leather seats and clean carpet. They had comfortable seats fit for a queen and that new-car smell that makes men swoon with envy.

For the first few years of their lives, these cars were kept in a tidy garage, washed and waxed every Saturday, and taken for long rides in the country every summer. They were loved and cherished and cared for.

But somewhere along the way they became neglected. The paint started to fade and the upholstery lost its luster. Eventually the cars became nothing more than piles of metal in the junkyard on the edge of town.

It's sad to see a car lose its purpose like that. But it's a tragedy of epic proportions when this happens to a marriage.

When God brings two souls together and binds them into one flesh, he considers that relationship a sacred and divine union, and he expects the couple to nurture that marriage to its full potential.

It's a sin to let our relationship with God get stale and lifeless and boring. It's also a sin to let our marriages get that way.

When God stepped in and saved our marriage, Karen and I had all but destroyed the love we once had for each other. Our harsh words and hardened hearts had beaten our love beyond recognition. I couldn't believe we had gone from two starry-eyed kids completely infatuated with each other to two disillusioned married people who could hardly stand to be in the same room. We not only lost our first love, but we could hardly remember what love felt like.

One of the key ways we resurrected those feelings of love was by doing the things we did at first. I began romancing Karen all over again. I began studying her again, looking for things she wanted to do and places she wanted to go. I started looking for ways to please her.

During the years that Karen and I were struggling in our marriage, one of her biggest complaints was the way I drove. I was no longer trying to impress her, so all the bad habits I had as a kid came back to the surface. I drove too fast, and when Karen complained, it made me angry and I'd drive even faster. I was young and immature and no longer cared what she thought.

So when it came time to start rekindling our romance, the first thing I knew I had to do was temper my driving. I began fighting the urge to speed, and I listened to Karen when she asked me to slow down. I even started using my blinkers again. I became the person she first fell in love with, because I was on a quest to regain the love we had lost.

A New Song

Psalm 98:1 tells us, "Sing to the LORD a new song, for he has done marvelous things."

Five times in the book of Psalms, King David encourages us to sing a new song to God because God is moved by creativity and imagination. God loves romance because it's a reflection of his own love for creation.

If you've found yourself strained and distant in your marriage, struggling to reconnect with your first love, let me encourage you to decide today to start singing a new song.

Take a long, deep breath and a big step back and determine once and for all to change the course of your future. Make a conscious decision of the will to take back the love you've lost, regardless of how far you've strayed or how deeply you've fallen. Commit today that you will no longer live in fear and frustration and uncertainty, that you will no longer settle for a bad marriage or even a good marriage. What you desire is a great marriage, an exceptional marriage—a long-lasting, exciting, dynamic love affair with your spouse. Then commit to start doing the things you did at first to get there.

Restoring Treasures

Not so long ago I attended an antique car show just to see if I could recognize some cars from my youth. I took just a short stroll down memory lane. I couldn't believe the quality of work that had been done on these old Fords and Chevys and Chryslers. Most of them looked better than they did the day they rolled out of the factory.

Every car on the line had bright new paint and fresh upholstery. Every inch of chrome was polished so high that it almost hurt your eyes to look directly at it. No matter which way you walked, that new-car smell permeated the air.

As I made my way up and down the aisles, I found myself losing track of time reminiscing about the good old days. When you love old cars as much as I do, it doesn't take much to get your nostalgic juices flowing.

I began imagining all the work that went into restoring these old classics. Every one of these cars could have easily ended up rusting in a farmer's field somewhere or piled up in the corner of a junkyard. But somewhere along the way, some caring mechanics found them tucked away in garages and saw something in them that everyone else had missed. Where most could see only beaten and battered old pieces of metal, those mechanics saw priceless treasures that had simply been neglected. So they took the cars home and started to work.

They began replacing old parts, sanding out paint, and fixing anything that needed to be fixed. They spent hour upon hour rebuilding, repairing, repainting, reupholstering, and refining. With surgeon-like skill they nurtured and cherished and cared for their newfound treasures.

Then one day they threw open the doors to their garages, and what emerged were things of beauty. The once rusted and neglected old cars had been restored to their full glory. And they couldn't wait to show off the transformation to others.

What If . . . ?

You know where I'm going with all this, don't you?

What if we all saw our marriages in that same light? What if we all applied that same level of care and commitment to bringing our marriages back to their full potential before God?

What if every wife started seeing her husband as the dashing young stud she once fell in love with instead of this gruff old guy who glares at her across the breakfast table? What if she started looking at him the way she once did, honoring him, praising him, cheering him on, encouraging him to become the person she knows he truly is?

And what if every husband began loving and cherishing and romancing his wife the way he once did, back when their love was young and fresh and exciting? What if he looked at her and saw only the beautiful treasure who had once captured his heart?

Do you think that would make a difference? Do you think God has enough lampstands in heaven to advertise all those great marriages?

I, for one, would really like to give it a try.

What about you?

14

Fearless Love

For God has not given us a spirit of fear, but of power and of love and of a sound mind.

2 Timothy 1:7 NKJV

There is no fear in love.

1 John 4:18

There are two deep-seated fears in the heart of every driven person.

The first is the fear of failure. You're afraid of not getting what you want. Afraid that you'll work your entire life toward a goal and still not get there. That after all your labor and toil, you'll come to the end of your days and discover that your labor was all in vain.

The second is the fear that you'll succeed, but it won't be what you expected. You fear that you'll get all the things you worked for, all the accomplishments you strove so hard to achieve—the big house, the fancy cars, the praise of your peers—and then wake up one morning to discover that you're just as empty and unsatisfied as before.

I understand these fears all too well, because I've always been an intensely driven person. There was a time when I could have been the poster child for the driven life. Even as a young man, I pushed myself to succeed. I knew what I wanted and I was determined to get there.

I don't consider this a badge of honor. This is a confession on my part, not a boast, because drivenness is not a healthy thing. Drivenness is rooted in fear and insecurity and doubt. It's a need to control your circumstances, and control is the natural enemy of faith. Control says, "I don't think God is big enough to handle my problems, so I need to handle them on my own." Control destroys relationships and sends families into a state of dysfunction.

Drivenness is not the same as diligence. Diligence is being dependable and competent and taking care of the things you need to take care of. Diligence is working hard to feed your family and preparing for the future. It is owning up to your responsibilities before God and then making the needed sacrifices to meet those obligations.

The difference between drivenness and diligence is that drivenness doesn't know when to stop.

A Driven Life

When our kids were growing up, one of my biggest struggles as a husband and father was keeping my priorities in order.

As the pastor of a large, fast-growing church, I found myself overwhelmed with responsibilities. There was never a moment when something didn't need to be done. When I wasn't preparing my Sunday lessons, I was counseling people in need, returning phone calls, meeting with the staff, or helping plan special events. I could have stayed at the building twenty-four hours a day and still found tasks that were being overlooked.

When Karen and I founded MarriageToday, life got even more demanding. Suddenly we found ourselves at the helm of a budding new ministry, and there was always work to be done. The ministry was started on a shoestring, and like any new venture, it constantly kept us on our toes. Things seldom went as planned, and new tasks were constantly rising to the surface. As the ministry grew, the stress increased exponentially.

God was at the helm of all these decisions, so we knew we were in his will. But as a driven person, I struggled daily to set boundaries and keep my priorities in order. I didn't always succeed. There were far too many nights when I was home with the family but my mind was still at work.

When our two kids were young, Karen and I always made a practice of having dinner together as a family. We'd gather around the table and have a family meal with no radio or television, and we'd each talk about our day, just like Karen and I did growing up. The idea was to spend time together as a family with no distractions, but often I was the one who missed the point. The stress of work would be weighing on my heart, and I'd be thinking of all the things I needed to be doing.

The kids would be talking about their day at school, telling some story about a funny thing that happened at lunch or recess, and everyone would be laughing and joining in the discussion. Everyone except me, that is. I'd be sitting quietly with my eyes glazed over.

Suddenly I would wake up and see my family staring at me. "Dad, where are you?" they'd say. "We've been talking for five minutes, and you haven't said a word." I would have no idea what they'd been talking about. My body was there, but I'd been far away, slaying dragons in another world.

Once Karen came to me after dinner and said, "Jimmy, your heart is not turned toward me and the kids. You're more interested in your work than you are in your family."

Her words hurt my feelings, and I told her she was wrong. I actually got pretty defensive about it. But in my heart I knew she was right. I had always struggled with drivenness, and my fear of failure was keeping me from being the husband and father my family needed me to be.

Thankfully, Karen was always there to hold me accountable. It always hurt when she reminded me that I was neglecting her and the kids, but it was something I needed to hear. I struggled with it throughout my life and prayed often that God would help me keep my priorities in order. With God's help, I did get better as time went on, but still today it's a battle I have to fight.

The Problem with Fear

When fear and worry come into our lives, they are always the work of Satan. His goal is to draw our attention away from God and onto ourselves.

Satan uses fear to destroy families, to weaken faith, to damage relationships, and to tear marriages apart. Fear is the enemy of trust and the destroyer of intimacy. Wherever you find fear, temptation is hiding nearby, waiting for a chance to pounce.

When Karen and I first married, our hearts were consumed with fear, and it very nearly destroyed our relationship.

Karen was deeply insecure and had an instinctive fear of rejection. She feared being devalued and disconnected from those she loved. Her fears only got worse because of the way I treated her. I was young and immature and riddled with fears of my own, so I tried to control her. I refused to open up emotionally and often treated her with disdain and disrespect, which made her feel even more insecure. She was dying inside, and I couldn't even see it.

My fears were so numerous and complex that it would take an entire book to describe the depth of my dysfunction as a husband. I had a deep fear of failure, which fueled my driven personality. I feared weakness and vulnerability, and those fears turned me into an emotional bully. I constantly overcompensated by pretending to be macho and strong and secure, but inside I was riddled with insecurity and doubt. I feared losing honor, so I dominated Karen and threw my weight around, just to make sure she knew who was in charge.

But perhaps my biggest fear was the fear of rejection. I was deeply afraid of losing Karen's love and respect, so I tried to hang on to her by keeping her under my thumb.

All of these fears weighed on our marriage, and Satan used them to try to tear us apart, knowing it's impossible to have intimacy in marriage when you're controlled by fear.

Back in chapter three I told the story of the night that I almost lost Karen for good. It was a defining moment in our marriage, because it was the first time I ever found the strength to overcome my fears and do the right thing. That event happened over thirty years ago, and I've told the story countless times since, because it truly was a turning point in our marriage.

After a huge fight, I found myself sitting alone in our living room as Karen cried uncontrollably in the bedroom. I had just told her to pack her bags and leave, and as I sat seething with rage, I suddenly realized that I was about to lose her forever. I knew I had finally pushed her too far and that if I didn't do something, our marriage would be over for good. My anger turned to shame and remorse, and I started to pray. "Lord, what have I done? I can't lose Karen. What am I supposed to do now?"

At that moment I instinctively knew that the only way I could save our marriage was to swallow my pride and apologize. I had to somehow summon the strength to overcome my fears and do the right thing. So I went into the other room, wrapped my arms around Karen, and told her I was sorry.

I didn't stop there. I apologized for all the times I had treated her with anger and disrespect, for all the hateful words I had said, for all the ways I had tried to dominate her, for all the insensitive and ungodly things I had ever said to her. I begged her to forgive me and give me another chance.

It was the first time I had ever humbled myself before Karen, and it took every ounce of strength within me to do so. I had finally taken control of my fears, and that decision saved our marriage.

Core Fears

Gary Smalley often talks about the "core fears" of men and women. He explains that we all have fears at the core of our lives that cause us to act out in hurtful and dysfunctional ways, and the core fears of women and men are different. Almost all struggles and insecurities in marriage can be traced to these basic core fears.

Women's fears are mostly related to disconnectedness. Women are relational by nature, and they often fear losing touch with the ones they love or being devalued in the marriage.

Men have a deep fear of dishonor and failure. They fear losing control. That's why so many men try to dominate their wives, as I once did. They fear being dominated and disrespected, so they compensate by trying to control others. This was my core fear in the early years of our marriage, and it is the core fear of almost all men as they enter into marriage.

I have a counselor friend who once told me about the biggest argument he and his wife had ever had. He was at work after a long day of counseling and getting ready to head home to his family. Just as he was about to leave his office, a young man showed up at his door. The man had just gone through a devastating event in his family, and he desperately needed to talk.

My friend put down his things and took the man back into his office to help. For several hours he counseled and comforted the young man through this difficult situation. It was an emotionally grueling evening for both of them, but through his wisdom he was able to defuse a dangerous situation. The man had been deeply depressed and suicidal and likely would have taken his own life if my friend hadn't been there to help.

After the young man left, my friend was feeling pretty good about the time he had spent helping, but he quickly realized that he had forgotten to call his wife. He knew she was waiting for him, so he made a quick phone call before heading home.

That's when it all happened. The minute she answered the phone, he could tell he was in trouble. "Where have you been?" she asked. "What have you been doing? Didn't you know I had supper waiting?"

She was so angry that he couldn't get a word in, and she had no interest in hearing his explanation. So he began to get angry as well. Finally he told her he'd explain when he got home, and he hung up the phone and headed to his car, still fuming at her impatience.

All the way home he thought about all the things he was going to say to her. "This man really needed me," he would tell her. "This is what I do! I help people! And you think supper is more important than that? Do you realize what could have happened? You should be proud of me, not worried about a little cold chicken!"

All the while she was at home preparing her speech. So by the time he walked in the front door, they were both loaded for bear and ready to go at it.

That evening quickly turned into the most bitter and agonizing fight of their marriage. The longer they fought, the more their anger escalated.

This kind of story is so common in marriage that it's almost predictable. It was a textbook case of two people acting out on their core fears and allowing those fears to get the best of them.

Her core fears were saying to her, "If he cared for me, he would have been home. If he loved me, he would have called earlier. He cares more about his job than he does his family."

His core fears were saying to him, "She doesn't respect me. She doesn't see the good I'm doing. Why doesn't she understand that my work is important?"

Their argument had nothing to do with counseling or cold food. It was all a reaction based on the deepest fears of their hearts. And the devil reached in and used those core fears to try to come between them.

Thankfully, they eventually worked through their differences and moved forward—something not all couples are able to do.

The Devil's Strategy

There is a reason Satan uses fear to tear families apart. There is a reason the enemy of our souls works so hard to discover the things we fear the most. It's because fear is the greatest enemy of faith. Faith and fear cannot coexist in the same heart. When one is present, the other is completely absent.

Fear says, "No one loves you. No one cares for you. You are all alone." Faith says, "You have a heavenly Father, and he cares about what happens to you. He will always be there, no matter what happens."

Fear says, "Your husband doesn't love you." "Your wife doesn't respect you." Faith says, "Respect your husband, even if you don't feel loved." "Love your wife, even when you don't feel respected."

Faith is believing that if we simply do the right thing, regardless of the circumstances, God will work everything out to his glory. Faith is knowing that we have no reason to fear, no reason to doubt, no reason to act out of insecurity and mistrust. Faith is understanding that we don't have to be in control, because God is. Because of that truth, the first and most critical step to overcoming fear is to give our fears to God. To put our full trust in God and allow him to be the security we need.

Like most matters of the Christian faith, that's much easier said than done. It isn't easy to let go of the things we fear the most. It isn't easy to turn our fears over to God and trust him to work things out. At the core of our hearts, we all are riddled with insecurity, and it isn't easy to let go.

I've been struggling with a need to control for all my life, and it is still a daily struggle for me. Because of that, Satan is constantly working to throw me off balance. The enemy knows that I am a driven person, so he continues to put boulders in my path that need moving. Every time I try to slow down my busy schedule, the devil dangles another task in front of me, constantly tempting me to push harder, to work longer, to stay busy.

Karen has always struggled with insecurity. Her greatest fear in our marriage has always been that I would become so immersed in work that I would neglect our family. She sees my drivenness, and it frightens her. She sees how busy I can get, and it tends to trigger her insecurities even more.

Because of these dueling fears, Satan has worked tirelessly to use my busy schedule to tear us apart.

Miles Away

This truth came home to roost in a sobering way just a few years ago during an exceptionally busy time in our ministry. It happened one night when our daughter, Julie, and her husband, Cory, were at our house visiting. They had asked us to babysit their twin daughters, Abby and Elle, and we never turn down a chance to be with our grandkids.

We were all at the house having a great time, laughing and talking, when I got a disturbing phone call. A good friend from work was going through a difficult situation, and I had been counseling him through it. He was having a very tough evening, and I was deeply concerned for him. It was a short phone conversation, but it weighed heavily on my heart. For most of the evening I was quiet and distracted. I tried hard to focus on my family and thought I was doing a good job of it, but apparently I wasn't very successful.

At one point I was standing alone, and Julie came to me and said, "Dad, what's wrong with you today? You're completely checked out."

"No, I'm not," I told her. "I'm a little concerned for my friend, but I'm here."

She didn't buy it. "No, you're not here," she told me. "You're miles away."

Then she said something that really convicted my heart.

"Dad, this is the way you were when I was little. You were home, but your mind was elsewhere. I don't want you to be that way with my daughters. They need a grandfather, and I want you to be there for them."

Her words weren't harsh, but they were steeped in concern. I knew she was right. It was like a heap of burning coals over my already convicted spirit. Once again I had been distracted by stress and worry and had started to neglect my family.

Karen came to me later that evening and told me the same thing. She got on me for being emotionally distant and preoccupied.

Then the Holy Spirit chimed in and sent a wave of guilt to pierce my heart and conscience. It was like a trinity of conviction. First Julie, then Karen, then God.

A Promise Renewed

That evening I recommitted to Karen that I would do whatever it took to keep my priorities in the right order and to be a doting and attentive father and grandfather. I spent time praying for supernatural strength and conviction. I promised God that I would once again slow down the pace of my life and trust him to take care of our ministry.

At the time, my speaking engagements were critical to the success of our television ministry. Speaking was how we raised money for the ministry and also how we grew our audience. It was an important part of keeping our bills paid and our staff employed.

But speaking also took me away from home far more often than I wanted, and I knew that Karen was frustrated with the amount of time I was spending on the road. She was patient, but she was also annoyed with my far-too-frenzied work schedule.

I promised God that I would learn to start saying no and trust him to bring in the money we needed to survive. I prayed, "Lord, by faith I am again putting our ministry in your hands, and I am putting you in charge of my schedule. I'm going to cut way back on speaking over the coming years, and I trust you to take care of our financial needs." I held true to that commitment, even though I could tell it worried our staff when I told them of my decision.

The very next week I got a call from a good friend who asked me to speak at an upcoming event he was planning, and I couldn't believe the offer he put on the table. He was a generous man, and the money he offered for this one speaking opportunity was more than I would normally make in ten speaking engagements. It was clear that God was blessing my commitment to slow down and trust.

Since that time God has continued to be faithful, far beyond our expectations. And I have continued to remain true to my word.

Often our ministry has succeeded in spite of me, not because of me. That is clearly because of God's hand of approval.

Letting Go of Fear

The Bible tells us, "For God has not given us a spirit of fear, but of power and of love and of a sound mind" (2 Tim. 1:7 NKJV). Whenever you find fear, you can bet the devil is behind it, because God never comes to us in fear. God dispels fear.

Whatever it is you fear the most is the one thing Satan will use to tear down your relationships, beginning with your marriage. Don't let that happen. Don't allow your fears to control you. Don't let Satan use your fears against you. Don't give in to the temptation to hold on to those things that are causing the most stress in your marriage.

Commit today to lay your fears at the feet of Jesus.

Lay down your need to control, your driven spirit, your doubts and insecurities. Lay down your need for honor and approval. Lay down your fear of rejection, your worries about tomorrow, your concerns for the future. Lay down the core fears of your heart and instead trust God to take care of your every need.

Intimacy cannot grow in a bed of fear. And intimacy is critical to a healthy, God-centered marriage.

Fear will consume your heart and devastate your marriage. Faith will comfort your heart and give your marriage the strength it needs to survive.

Fear will tear you down. Faith will build you up.

Fear is Satan's playground. Faith is God's comforting shelter of love.

We all are controlled by one or the other—faith or fear. And where we put our trust has a greater impact on our marriage than we can possibly comprehend.

15

Covenantal Love

We promised to work to stay together not because
we think things between us will never change, but
because we know they will.

Eric Zorn

Never will I leave you; never will I forsake you.

Hebrews 13:5

When I was a kid, people were very loyal to businesses.
You would shop at the same grocery store, get your
tools at the local Ace Hardware, go to the same bar-
ber when you needed a haircut, and buy your meat from the corner
butcher. You got to know the people who ran these stores, and you
actually looked forward to seeing them. You'd feel guilty if you went
anywhere else. The community you lived in felt like a community.
That's why every person within ten blocks of my house thought
they could raise me, because they all knew who I was—and what I
wasn't supposed to be doing.

Today that's no longer the case. Big-box stores have largely replaced the corner markets. Instead of buying from the local shops, we're all looking for the best deals and the most convenient ways to shop. These days you can get a can of beans and a hammer at the same store, and even pick up a new mattress on your way out the door.

Major retailers are constantly vying for our business, and they know exactly how to get it. They study us, watch our buying habits, learn our tipping points, and use what they've learned to lure us in.

From a budget standpoint, that's not always a bad thing. Competition means lower prices, so it's easier on our wallets. But on the downside, we're all less connected than we once were. And we're far less loyal. Marketers know that all they have to do to gain our business is offer us a better deal, a slightly better product, and a quicker transaction. Devotion to our community has given way to a shopper's mentality.

I'm all in favor of saving a few bucks, so I'm not complaining. There's nothing wrong with having a shopper's mentality in the marketplace, because it keeps businesses on their toes. The trouble comes when we take that same mentality into a relationship. A shopper's mentality in marriage is a devastating thing.

Today you can go on the internet and buy anything you need. You can also go on the internet and find anyone you want, like chat partners, people who share your interests and hobbies, even long-lost friends and acquaintances from high school. Whatever it is you enjoy doing, you can find people online who enjoy doing it just as much as you.

You can even find old girlfriends and boyfriends.

The internet can be an exciting place to shop and play and visit. But it can also be a breeding ground for trouble when your heart and eyes start to stray.

A Shopper's Mentality

Not so long ago I had a woman in my office who was sobbing uncontrollably. She was an attractive woman in her fifties, and she wept from the moment she sat down in the chair across from me. She could hardly get a sentence out between her cries of anguish.

She told me how her husband was constantly looking at other women no matter where they went. In restaurants he couldn't keep his eyes from wandering around the room. When a young woman walked by their table, he would ogle her. While driving down the street, he would stare at women on the sidewalk. He even noticed billboards and posters. Everywhere they went, his eyes were constantly roaming. And he would make comments about these other women, regularly comparing them to his wife. Often his words were in jest, but they were deeply hurtful just the same.

This poor woman was devastated by her husband's wandering eye. He had all but destroyed her battered self-esteem.

When we bring a shopper's mentality into our marriage, we're saying to our partner, "If you don't meet my needs, I can find someone else who will. If you don't give me what I want, I'll find it elsewhere. Somewhere out there is a better mate, and if I find them, I may be gone for good."

A shopper's mentality destroys any sense of loyalty and commitment in the marriage. Our partner becomes just another commodity. Just one of many products on the shelf to choose from. No different than a piece of property or a head of lettuce.

A shopper's mentality gives us the right to shop around when we're not happy, to compare different makes and models, to consider stopping at the big-box store across town instead of staying loyal to the corner grocer. It gives us the right to look at other women, to flirt with other men, to compare our partner with others in the marketplace.

A shopper's mentality is devastating to a relationship, and it will destroy a marriage faster than just about any other social and relational dynamic.

Where It Came From

Where does this shopper's mentality come from?

Simply put, it comes from a humanistic, secularized view of marriage. It comes from a nonscriptural, anti-Christian worldview. It comes from a church that has allowed secular humanism to infiltrate its theology.

It was a problem when Jesus walked the earth, and it's still a problem today.

Once Jesus was teaching and healing in Judea when a group of Pharisees asked him, "Is it lawful for a man to divorce his wife for any and every reason?" (Matt. 19:3).

Their words were meant to test Jesus, but that wasn't their only objective. The religious leaders of the day knew well what Scripture had to say about marriage and divorce, but they had long since come up with their own rules and regulations on the matter. Women were seen as property, and their religious laws reflected that view. All a man had to do to divorce his wife was to hand her a piece of paper and say three times, "I divorce you," and the marriage was over. She would have to leave without her children, without any belongings, and without an ounce of dignity. Often these women were killed for shaming their families.

The Pharisees were the ones who had come up with these rules. Though they professed to follow Scripture, their views were categorically secular and humanistic.

Jesus saw through the charade and said to them, "Haven't you read . . . that at the beginning the Creator 'made them male and female,' and said, 'For this reason a man will leave his father and mother and be united to his wife, and the two will become one flesh'? . . . Therefore what God has joined together, let no one separate" (vv. 4–6).

Jesus was saying to them, "You know what God thinks about marriage. He sees it as a sacred covenant. In God's eyes, marriage is a lifelong, unbreakable commitment."

But in spite of what the Scriptures taught, the Pharisees had already assumed a secular worldview of marriage, and that view permeated and perverted their theology. They embraced a twisted, humanistic understanding of marriage, and because of it, they had developed a shopper's mentality.

The Seven-Year Itch

Years ago there was a movie starring Marilyn Monroe called *The Seven Year Itch*. The story is about a man who is seven years into his marriage and beginning to get bored and restless. When his family leaves town for the summer, he becomes infatuated with a beautiful young neighbor and starts to fantasize about having an affair.

The idea came from a school of thought that's been around longer than any of us can remember. Because most divorces occurred around the seventh year of marriage, someone in history coined the phrase "seven-year itch," and it just stuck. Seven years appeared to be the point at which many people started reevaluating their relationships, and marriages that lasted beyond that point were thought to be pretty solid and secure.

Today sociology professors in major universities actually teach this dynamic as part of their curriculum. They teach that marriage works better and people are happier if they change spouses every seven years. They claim that we are genetically wired by evolution to need a major change in our lives every seven years or so, and what could be more major than changing spouses?

It's the epitome of secular humanistic philosophy, yet it's being packaged and peddled to our kids as enlightened intellectual reasoning. Even more disturbing, this type of thinking is infiltrating our churches. More than at any other time in history, Christians are buying into a secular worldview.

One recent poll showed that the majority of believers no longer base their major moral decisions on what the Bible says but instead on what they believe will bring the best results. They consider the Bible to be a good source of teaching and history but culturally outdated. So instead they turn to "common sense" and reasoning when making critical life choices.

Ever wonder why the divorce rate among believers is only a fraction different than it is among nonbelievers?

The Three Components of Covenant

Marriage works only on the basis of covenant. And covenant is God's idea. Marriage wasn't invented by a lonely group of Neanderthals in a cave somewhere. It was designed by God as a lifelong, supernaturally binding promise between a man and a woman.

You don't make a covenant by signing a marriage license and saying the right words. You make a covenant through a sacred and binding oath. You invoke your covenant knowing it will involve pain and sacrifice and commitment. And then you seal that covenant with a sign, a consecrated seal of exclusivity and permanence.

Covenant is a solemn agreement between two people, before God, and in the company of witnesses, and it's not something you enter into lightly. It is the most powerful and binding agent on earth. Treating it any other way is a mockery to God and a monumental breach of faith.

Covenant is the cornerstone of marriage. It is the foundation on which every other aspect of the relationship is built. Without covenant, you are just two people sleeping in the same bed and sharing living expenses. It's covenant that holds you together through both thick and thin times.

Every covenant has three distinct and critical components. Without these components, it's not a covenant, just another promise. These elements are essential to the fulfillment of a covenant, and together they create a connection that is deeply spiritual and eternally significant. It is these components that set a covenant apart from any other human agreement.

The three components of a covenant include a sacred oath, a sign and a seal, and a sacrifice.

A Sacred Oath

All covenants begin with a sacred and binding oath. This is the first component of any covenant, and it is actually the basis on which the covenant is made. If it weren't for promises that needed to be kept, there would be no reason for the covenant.

I've performed a lot of weddings through the years, and I honestly don't think I've ever seen a bride and groom who fully understood the weight of the vows they were making—particularly when they were young and "in love."

I had no idea what I was getting into when I stood next to Karen in front of the preacher. I was just hoping my hair looked good and that Karen wouldn't come to her senses and make a mad dash for the back door while she still had a chance.

Often when I counsel couples before their wedding, I'll ask if they've prepared any vows they'd like to exchange. Usually I get a vacant stare. They've spent months planning every aspect of the ceremony and know exactly what music they want to play, what kind of flowers they want, what they want to wear, even where they want to stand, but when it comes to the vows, they draw a complete blank. They usually just assume that it's the preacher's job to bring the vows. They've put more thought into the color scheme than they have into the binding promises they're about to make.

But wedding vows are actually the centerpiece of the ceremony. Without the vows, a wedding is little more than a really expensive party, because the vows are what make it such a sacred and solemn event.

The promises a bride and groom make at their wedding ceremony are likely the most sobering and humbling words they will ever utter.

A groom takes his bride's hand, looks her in the eye, and promises to stand by her side from that moment on, no matter what the future holds. He vows to be there for her, even if it means living in poverty, even if she gets sick, even if everything around them completely falls apart. He promises never to look at another woman, to give up his friends and family for her, to give her all he is and all he has, and to love and cherish her, no matter how hard she is to love and cherish. He promises to do all this until his very last breath.

Then the bride looks her groom in the eye and makes that same vow.

This is a staggering commitment to make to another person. This promise is for all the marbles. No gambler would lay down that many chips on one hand, no matter what cards he held.

Yet this is the commitment that couples make when they choose to get married, because marriage is the ultimate pledge of sacrifice and submission to another person. Only our surrender to God holds more weight and conviction.

A Sign and a Seal

The second component of a covenant is a sign and a seal.

Wherever you find covenant, you find an outward sign that seals it. The sign binds the commitment and reminds you that you have a covenantal partner.

After God flooded the earth, he promised Noah that he would never again destroy the earth with water, and to seal his promise he gave a rainbow. Whenever you see a rainbow in the sky, you are reminded of this covenant. You can be completely certain that no matter how hard it rains, no matter how much territory the water covers, God will eventually stop the rain from falling.

When God made a covenant with Abraham, he promised to make his descendants as vast and numerous as the stars in the sky. His sign to seal that covenant was circumcision. He commanded that every male descendant of Abraham, both present and future, be circumcised as a reminder of his promise, beginning with Abraham himself.

Wouldn't you love to have been a fly on the wall during that conversation? I'm sure Abraham was thrilled with the blessing, but the foreskin thing? I'm not sure any of them were prepared for that one. But this is how God chose to signify and seal his covenant with Abraham.

Today the covenantal seal of salvation is water baptism. It is the sign that signifies our surrender to God and our decision to follow Christ. We show our commitment by physically reenacting the death, burial, and resurrection of Jesus. It is an outward display of our willingness to die to self and be resurrected with Christ.

Baptism is the seal of our new covenant with Christ, and the sign of that covenant is communion. We regularly partake of the elements to remind us of our promise. Communion is a symbol of Christ's sacrifice for our sins. The bread and the wine are symbols of his body and blood poured out for us on the cross to save us. Through water baptism and communion, not only do we signify our commitment to Christ, but we share in the blessings he promised to those who choose to follow him.

Within the covenant of marriage, there is also a seal and a sign.

Whenever I ask people what they think the covenant sign is in marriage, they point to their wedding ring. We instinctively think of the ring because it's the most obvious outward sign of marriage. I like the idea of a wedding ring, and I wear mine proudly because I want women to know that my heart is already taken, but it's not the covenant sign of marriage. The ring wasn't God's idea.

The covenant sign of marriage is sex. We consummate our covenant through sexual intimacy. Each time we enter the marriage bed, we are remembering the commitment we made to each other.

Through sexual intimacy we are saying to our spouse, "I remember that I selected you among all others, and I believe that God brought us together. I am here to meet your needs and to honor God, and I am choosing to be faithful to you. I give myself to you, and only to you, for the rest of my days on earth."

Sex is a sacred and binding sign of our covenantal promise. Each time we engage in sex, we are reestablishing our commitment to each other.

This is why sexual sins are such an affront to God. He takes covenant very seriously. The apostle Paul wrote:

> Flee from sexual immorality. All other sins a person commits are outside the body, but whoever sins sexually, sins against their own body. Do you not know that your bodies are temples of the Holy Spirit, who is in you, whom you have received from God? You are not your own; you were bought at a price. Therefore honor God with your bodies.
>
> 1 Corinthians 6:18–20

All sins are offensive to God, but sexual sins are held up as an even greater offense. When you sin sexually, you are sinning against your body, which is no longer yours. Your body belongs to God and to your spouse. When you sin sexually, you are breaking covenant. And breaking covenant is a dangerous thing when dealing with a covenantal God.

God blesses those who faithfully keep their covenants, and he sternly disciplines those who don't. We see that truth played out in Scripture, and it should serve as a stark reminder to us whenever we are tempted to fall.

This doesn't mean that God won't forgive sexual sins. We all are sinful, and God is a forgiving God. He has promised to remain faithful even when we are faithless. But it does mean that we need to develop a special kind of sensitivity toward sexual sins and do whatever we need to do to guard against them. Sexual intimacy is a covenantal seal, and it is reserved exclusively for the marriage bed.

A Sacrifice

The third component of covenant is sacrifice. By its very definition, a covenant is a sacred commitment, and all commitments involve a level of self-sacrifice.

The word *covenant* literally means "to cut." You don't *make* covenant, you *cut* covenant. When God created marriage, he cut Adam's side. Adam bled real blood as a sacrifice for the covenant. When many women have sex for the first time, they bleed, and it's no accident that women were designed that way. It is symbolic of the serious and sacrificial nature of the marital covenant.

Through our marriage vows, we are making the ultimate commitment of self. We are promising to completely empty ourselves on behalf of our spouse.

In marriage, we say to our mate, "I promise to invest all I am and all I have in taking care of your needs and desires. I promise to put your needs ahead of my own. I commit to sacrificing my own dreams and desires to help you fulfill yours. I give myself to you completely, without reserve and without hesitation."

This is the most selfless and sacrificial commitment a person can make to another person. When we vow to stay with our partner "for better or for worse, in good times and bad times, in sickness and in health," we are saying to them, "I know that inevitable trials are ahead. I know things won't always go as planned. I know there will be sickness, times of stress and trouble, times of testing and frustration, times of turmoil and chaos, times when being married to you won't be much fun at all, but even so, I commit to staying with you, no matter what. I sacrifice my future for you."

Marriage is a sacrificial covenant. The greater the sacrifice, the more binding and sacred and rewarding the covenant becomes.

I've seen hundreds of great marriages in my life, and what I've discovered is that the best marriages are not those that somehow escape trials and tribulations. The best marriages are made up of two people who have gone through tremendous struggles and yet refused to let those struggles tear them apart. They've been through the trenches together and have suffered through sickness and poverty and hardship, yet they've clung to each other in the midst of it to make it through. They've been to hell and back in their marriage and come out even stronger than before.

The best marriages are those that have been tested and hardened by fire—those that have sacrificed the most to stay true to the marriage covenant.

The Power of Covenant

You and I are living in dangerous times. Marriage today is under assault in ways that many of us could never have imagined just a few short years ago. The temptations to stray have never been greater. And the availability of sin—as well as the acceptance of sin—has never been more pronounced.

Keeping covenant has never been more difficult. That's the bad news.

The good news is, when you've succeeded in staying true to your covenant—in spite of the struggles, in spite of all the trials and tribulations that have come against you, in spite of the temptations Satan has put in your path—you have accomplished something very near and dear to the heart of God. And when you move God's heart, blessings always follow.

God has promised us, "Never will I leave you; never will I forsake you" (Heb. 13:5). That is a covenant of monumental proportions, one that frees us from any hint of fear or worry for the future. It's a promise that is binding and secure and nonnegotiable. God has promised to be faithful, no matter what happens.

I haven't always lived worthy of God's love. I've given him hundreds, even thousands, of reasons to forsake me, yet he has always been there. He has never once turned away, even for a moment.

That's the power of covenant. Covenant is sacred and sacrificial and without condition. It is a commitment to stay true to a promise, regardless of how you might feel or what the other person does. That's the promise we make when we choose to live in covenant with another person.

Several years ago Karen went through a season of sickness. For several months she struggled with poor health, and her sickness made her weak and frail. I did all I could to comfort her, but it was a very trying time in her life. She couldn't do much around the house and needed more sleep than usual. We were all concerned because her illness hung on longer than any of us expected, and it took a terrible toll on her body. We trusted God to bring her through it, but it was a difficult season for Karen.

During this time I did all I could to take up the slack. I tried to take care of the house and the kids and the cooking and whatever else needed to be done. I honestly was happy to do it, but Karen really struggled with the idea of being so helpless. We weren't able to be sexually intimate very often during this time, and she continued to feel bad about that.

One night she came to me with tears in her eyes and apologized for her sickness. "I'm so sorry I've been so helpless," she said. "I'm sorry I can't be there for you at night. I feel terrible that I've been neglecting you and the kids." As usual, Karen was more concerned about her family than she was about her own well-being.

I took her in my arms, held her, and said, "Karen, you know how much I love you. You know how many years we've been together and how many times you have stood by my side and loved me. You don't have to worry about me. I'm not going to shop around. You don't have to do anything to earn my love. I just want you to stay in bed and get well. My heart is never going to stray. I love you, Karen. And I'll always love you, no matter what."

That's the beauty of a covenant relationship. It isn't a promise that's tied to performance or bound by stipulations. It isn't a contractual agreement. It is a willful commitment of the heart with no strings attached. No ulterior motives. No hidden agendas. No preconceived schemes or objectives. No fine print in the margins. No shopper's mentality when things get tough.

It's a willingness to put your own needs and desires on the back burner and instead focus on the needs of another. It's a dogged determination of the will to be true to the promises you made, regardless of what others might do, in spite of what society might say, no matter what temptations may come your way.

Covenant love is living in complete safety and security with another person. It is saying to them, "I don't know what the future holds. I don't know what forces may try to come between us. But I will never leave you or forsake you. My life and my heart are yours from this day forward. You can be certain that I will be there when you wake up in the morning, and the day after that, and every day for the rest of your life. No matter what happens, you are stuck with me, and that will never change."

16

The Journey of Love

May your fountain be blessed, and may you rejoice
in the wife of your youth.

Proverbs 5:18

It is good to have an end to journey towards; but it
is the journey that matters in the end.

Ursula K. LeGuin

Years ago I attended a men's retreat and heard speaker Roy
Hicks Jr. He was talking about the misguided ways we pri-
oritize our lives, and he made a statement that deeply convicted my spirit. He said, "The journey is the destination." Then
he explained that most men are convinced that the purpose of their
lives is to reach some lofty goal or achieve some great accomplishment, so they set their sights on a target and spend their days trying
to reach it. They become so driven to reach this elusive destination
that they completely neglect the most important people in their lives
along the way.

He went on to explain that the true purpose and meaning of a man's life is found in the journey, not the destination. The point of life is not where we're going but how we get there and who we get there with. Once our eternal fate with Christ is sealed, our destination is in God's hands. Our job is to focus on the present and live each day in God's will.

At the time I was a textbook case of the very guy Roy was talking about. I was constantly looking forward, reaching for another goal, driving toward another accomplishment. That's why his words burned into my heart and spirit. As a driven personality, I had spent far too much of my life setting goals and then striving to reach them.

More than any man in the room, I needed to hear his lesson.

The Problem of Worry

God isn't impressed with the accomplishments you achieve, the money you accumulate, the clothes you wear, or the houses and cars you own. He's not impressed by the businesses you've run, the churches you've pastored, or the ministries you've been able to develop. It's not the goals you've set or the great things you've accomplished that get his attention.

With God, it's about the relationships you've nurtured along the way. It's about the priorities you've established. It's about character and integrity. It's about the primary focus of your life.

God is far more interested in seeing faithful hearts, healthy families, and strong marriages than large bank accounts or achieved goals.

Jesus told his disciples, "Do not worry about your life, what you will eat or drink; or about your body, what you will wear. Is not life more than food, and the body more than clothes?" (Matt. 6:25).

The reason worry is so offensive to God is because it destroys relationships. It destroys our relationship with him as well as with the people he puts into our lives. When we obsess over money and goals and the future, we lose track of what's most important. When we worry, we are saying to God, "I don't think you're big enough. I don't think you care enough to take care of me. I don't trust you to be there when I need you."

Worry is the natural enemy of trust. And without trust, it's impossible to have a relationship with God.

Jesus said, "So do not worry, saying, 'What shall we eat?' or 'What shall we drink?' or 'What shall we wear?' . . . But seek first his kingdom and his righteousness, and all these things will be given to you as well" (Matt. 6:31, 33).

"Let me worry about tomorrow," Jesus tells us. "You enjoy the journey and put your trust in me, and all your needs will be taken care of."

In God's economy, the journey is the destination, because it's only in the journey that we learn to appreciate the true blessings of life.

Chasing Success

Dr. James Dobson once told the story of the first time he ever went golfing. He said he had never had an interest in the sport, but he decided to try it since so many of his friends played and were often bugging him to join them.

As he drove up to the course that day, he was struck by the sheer beauty of the landscape. The course was perfectly manicured, with old trees, fresh flowers, rolling hills, and newly mown grass as far as the eye could see. It was a beautifully tended golf course, and just walking up to the first tee lifted his spirit.

But then it came time to tee off, and suddenly everything changed. He swung as hard as he could and caught the ball on the toe of the club, slicing it into the tall grass about fifty feet in front of him. He took out an iron and strolled over to hit it again, but his second shot wasn't much better. This time the ball ended up in the woods, in even taller grass.

His third shot was a bit better, but his ball still came to rest in a bed of weeds. His fourth shot took him all the way to the other side of the fairway, behind several large trees.

This pattern went on for the entire first hole, until finally he landed his ball on the green. Even then it took another four strokes to get it into the hole. He said he had taken so many swings that he didn't even bother to count them, just picked up his ball and made his way to the second tee.

This second hole wasn't any better.

Dr. Dobson described his day on the course as the most frustrating afternoon of his life. He spent the entire time chasing a little white ball around the course, trying his best to get it headed in the right direction. He chased it back and forth across the greens, in and out of the woods, through sand traps and behind trees, even into several creek beds.

He finished the round that day completely exhausted from the hunt. He felt utterly beaten and discouraged, so he said good-bye to his friends and hurried back to his car, hoping to salvage at least part of his day doing something productive.

As he was driving away, he glanced back at the course one last time and once again was struck by the sheer beauty of it all. He realized that he had just spent much of his day on one of the most beautiful golf courses in the country, yet he never once took time to stop and appreciate it. He was so focused on getting that stupid white ball into the hole that he completely lost sight of the scenery along the way.

What was intended to be an enjoyable and relaxing afternoon with a few of his buddies ended up being an exercise in futility and frustration.

Isn't that how life can be sometimes? How often have you and I done the same thing? So many of us spend our entire lives chasing after some elusive little ball, and we completely lose sight of the beauty surrounding us on every side. We're so focused on reaching the next goal, on getting that big promotion, on finishing our degree, on growing our company, on building our ministry, on writing our next book, that we don't even see the most important things in our lives. We completely miss the blessings that are right in front of our eyes.

When Time Is Lost

When our kids were young, we had a blue couch in our den. It was a great couch, but it needed to be replaced because it had orange stains all over the cushions. Our son, Brent, had a strange addiction to Cheetos, and he always ate on that couch when we watched television together as a family.

It used to drive me nuts to see him wiping his hands all over our blue couch, but after a while it became a lost cause to complain, because the damage had already been done. I decided just to bite my tongue and live with it, at least until the kids left home.

It wasn't long before Brent went away to college. It was an exciting time in his life but a difficult transition for Karen and me. I took it much harder than I thought I would. My son was growing up and leaving home, and though I knew it was a healthy transition, the dad in me really struggled to let go.

One day just a few weeks after he'd left, I walked past our blue couch and saw those unsightly orange stains, and without warning tears started welling up in my eyes. I began to cry. I remembered all the times Brent used to sit on that couch munching on Cheetos, and I thought, *I'd give anything to have him back here again. I wish he was still here, still living at home, still laughing and running through the halls, still messing up his room and playing his loud music. Still wiping his greasy fingers all over that stupid couch.*

The longer we live, the faster time flies, and the more we wish we could do it all again. The more we wish we could hug our kids once more, throw the ball with them, take them to the movies, tuck them into bed one last time before they grow up and have families of their own.

The longer we live, the more we treasure the years we've spent with our spouse. We wish we could go back in time and relive it. We would take them on more dates, give them more love and attention, spend more time curled up on the couch with them, take more long walks in the woods, tell them more often how much they mean to us.

The longer we live, the more precious these ordinary moments become to us. The more we realize how important it is to slow down in life and enjoy the journey.

The Cleaving Principle

When God brought Adam and Eve together in marriage, he said, "Therefore shall a man leave his father and his mother, and shall *cleave* unto his wife" (Gen. 2:24 KJV, italics mine).

The Old Testament word for *cleave* is an active word, filled with effort and emotion. It's a purposeful word, a dynamic word, a passionate word. It's a word that conveys great energy, as in "to climb a mountain" or "to pursue a relationship with zeal and passion."

Men are commanded to *cling* to their wives, to pursue them, to be fully connected with them. And it's not possible to passively cling to someone. It takes work and sweat to hang on, to stay bound together, to keep from drifting apart. You have to grab hold and refuse to let go.

Cleaving can happen only in the present. You can't cleave to someone in the past or the future. It can be done only in the here and now. To cleave to someone, you have to be fully engaged in the activity, fully alive to the task, fully aware of the things that can easily pull you apart.

In many ways, marriage is like being in two rowboats in the middle of a vast and tumultuous ocean and trying desperately to keep your boats together. Your job is to stay side by side as you navigate the turbulent seas of life. The only way it will work is if you cling together. You have to grab hold of each other and not let go. Otherwise you can easily get separated.

When the storms come, holding on takes even greater effort. You literally have to bind your boats together to keep them from being ripped apart by the unbridled winds and waves of life. It is a struggle, a wild and reckless brawl, a battle of epic proportions, to stay together when the hurricanes of life come at you, hell-bent on ripping you apart.

You'll lose the battle if your head isn't in the game. If your mind is focused on the past or dreaming of the future, you'll lose the fight that faces you in the present.

Relationships work only in the here and now. Families function only when everyone is focused on the moment. Marriage demands your full attention to the struggles of today. You have to stop obsessing over the future and be fully engaged in the journey.

So many people are convinced that attraction is what keeps a marriage strong. They believe that chemistry and magnetism are what bind people together and turn them into "soul mates." But if that were true, you would never hear of a divorce coming out of Hollywood. The most beautiful people in the country gather together in one spot to make movies, and many of them hook up like alley cats. If chemistry could make a good marriage, they'd be the most faithful people on the planet.

You and I both know that isn't the case. There's a reason divorce lawyers own some of the biggest mansions in Hollywood.

What keeps a marriage solid are energy and commitment. It takes a dogged determination of the will to cling together, no matter what struggles you may face. It takes a decision of the heart and soul to allow God to bind your lives together into one flesh. It takes two people saying to each other, "Nothing is going to take your place. Not today. Not tomorrow. Not ever. I'm going to cleave to you, to cling to you, to relentlessly pursue you until my last breath. Only my relationship with God is going to take precedence over our marriage. No storm, no tempest, no temptation, no amount of pain or distress will ever tear us apart."

"What Is Sexy?"

A certain commercial ran on television a few years ago that offended me deeply. It was so degrading to women that I couldn't believe it was allowed to run.

It was a lingerie commercial for a large, national retail chain, and it began with a pencil-thin, scantily clad model sitting in a chair. Across the screen came the words "What is sexy?" The next thing viewers saw was a series of images flashing across the screen. Each image depicted a different woman perfectly shaped and posing seductively for the camera, each one wearing a different type and color of lingerie.

I was offended not only by the blatantly sexual nature of the commercial but by the distorted message it was relaying. "What is sexy?" the commercial asked. And then it answered that question by parading a handful of surgically enhanced, desperately underfed supermodels across the screen.

It's no wonder so many marriages feel strained. No wonder so many women struggle with deep feelings of doubt and insecurity. The world has set the standard so high that no woman could possibly measure up.

I can't imagine what it's like to be a woman living in a sex-crazed, supermodel-worshiping world. I can't imagine what it feels like to go through life constantly comparing yourself with other women, most of them half your age, and then wondering if your husband is doing the same thing.

Job set an example for every husband when he said, "I made an agreement with my eyes. I promised not to look at another woman with sexual longing" (Job 31:1 NIrV).

Karen knows that she is the most beautiful woman in the world to me. No one will ever compare. And she gets more beautiful with each passing year. When she is a hundred years old, she will officially be the sexiest hundred-year-old woman I've ever seen. Not to mention much easier to catch.

Karen knows I have eyes only for her and that she will always captivate my heart. She knows this because I make a point of telling her at every opportunity.

I will never dishonor Karen by comparing her to another woman, because no other woman has stood by my side the way she has. No other woman has gone through the pain of bearing my children, the sacrifice of raising them, the struggle of staying true to our marriage through all of Satan's attempts to tear us apart. No other woman has seen the depth and breadth of my flaws and chosen to love me in spite of them.

No other woman has traveled through the storms of life with me, fought in the trenches with me, traveled to hell and back with me, and stayed by my side through every minute of the journey.

"Rejoice in the wife of your youth," said the writer of Proverbs. "May her breasts satisfy you always, may you ever be intoxicated with her love" (Prov. 5:18–19).

So what is sexy?

I'll tell you what sexy *isn't*. It isn't a degrading, airbrushed image on the cover of a magazine. It isn't a handful of seductive models pouting in their underwear on television.

Sexy is a woman who takes her groom's hand at the altar and pledges to stay by his side, no matter what the future holds. No matter how poor or fat or old he gets. No matter how sick he gets. No matter how many storms life throws in their path. Sexy is a woman who promises to love and honor her husband in spite of his many flaws and weaknesses and then spends her life staying true to that promise.

Sexy is a man who stands next to his bride and pledges to love and cherish her, to forsake all other women, to be there for her through thick and thin, to cling to her side as they navigate the tempests of life together. Then he spends every waking moment fulfilling that commitment.

Sexy is two flawed but determined souls who devote their lives to making each other happy. Two people committed to staying together, to meeting each other's needs, to being there when all others have turned away. To loving and honoring each other, no matter what struggles come into their lives.

Sexy is a love that survives against all odds. A love that is orchestrated and blessed by God and built on the principles he established.

Sexy is a love that lasts a lifetime.

The Story of Mike and Kathy

I began this book with the story of Walter and Lisa. It was a sad story about a marriage that ended in a devastating divorce. Walter was a man who refused to keep his commitment to God and his family, and because of it, he brought untold pain and chaos into the lives of his wife and children.

Before closing, I'd like to share another story with you—this one a story of triumph and recommitment. It's the story of Mike and Kathy.

Mike was a popular singer and entertainer with a lot of talent and a fast-growing fan base, and Kathy was his wife of ten years. They had four beautiful kids and were extremely active in their local church. Kathy was a stay-at-home mom who spent a lot of evenings at home with the kids while Mike traveled with his band.

Mike was a godly and sincere Christian and even served as a deacon in their church, but his career brought on a lot of temptation to sin. As the lead singer of a band, Mike often had young, starry-eyed groupies coming on to him. He was committed to staying faithful, but the more he traveled, the harder he found that to do.

One night an attractive woman in the front row at his concert was somehow able to slip Mike a note with a key to a hotel room attached. He laughed and slipped the key into his pocket, thinking he'd give it back to her after the concert. *Why would I throw away my marriage for one night of passion?* he thought. But the more she flirted with her eyes, the weaker his resolve became. That night temptation got the best of him, and for the first time in his marriage, Mike was unfaithful to his wife.

Over the coming months, the guilt of that night weighed heavily on Mike's heart. He felt terrible for what he had done. His biggest fear was that Kathy would find out. But she never did. She never suspected anything. Eventually Mike was able to breathe easy, convinced that he had gotten away with his sin.

It wasn't long before Mike was faced with another opportunity to stray, and once someone has fallen to sexual sin, the second time comes much easier. Again he was unfaithful, and again he suffered through several more months of guilt and remorse.

The third one-night stand was even easier. And then he fell a fourth time. Then a fifth. Then several more after that.

Kathy never suspected that her husband was being unfaithful, but she sensed that something wasn't quite right. They began to fight more than usual, and Mike began developing a temper—something he'd never had a problem with in the past. The two of them found themselves fighting over even the smallest issues. Soon their marriage was thrown into a state of constant turmoil.

What Kathy didn't know was that Mike was being eaten up with guilt. Each time he fell into sin, the shame would gnaw at his conscience, sending him into fits of anger and self-loathing. He knew he needed to stop, but he didn't have the strength under his own power. And the more he strayed, the more he and Kathy struggled to get along.

Finally Mike realized that he had to confess to Kathy. Otherwise he would never be able to take the steps he needed to stay faithful to their marriage. He didn't know how Kathy would react to his confession or even if their marriage could survive it; he only knew that he could no longer keep this dark secret hidden from her.

So one night he sat across the table from his wife and told her what he had done.

Kathy was devastated. Neither of them knew how they would ever get past the pain and move forward. Kathy never imagined she'd have to deal with such a monumental breach of trust. But they were committed to doing whatever it took to keep their marriage together.

Though money was tight, they began seeing a good counselor on a weekly basis. They even sold one of their cars to help pay for it. They were determined to rebuild their strained marriage, no matter how much it might cost them.

Mike began surrounding himself with Christian friends and mentors who were willing to hold him accountable. He confessed to his pastor and the elders of their church, asking them to pray for him and be there for him when he needed to talk. Then he threw himself into daily prayer and Bible study.

It took Mike and Kathy several years of work and sacrifice to rebuild their marriage, but through their dedication, God did a miracle in their relationship. He didn't just save their marriage; he helped them build a bond that was far deeper and stronger than they had ever experienced before.

Today Mike and Kathy have the marriage of their dreams. Their relationship is stronger today than either of them ever imagined it could be. And a lot of their time is spent mentoring other couples who have been shaken by infidelity. Their marriage is a powerful testament to what God can do in a relationship when we look to him for healing.

What Satan set out to destroy, God instead remade into a thing of beauty.

A God of Restoration

God promised the nation of Israel through the prophet Joel, "I will restore to you the years that the swarming locust has eaten" (Joel 2:25 NKJV). Each time the Israelites repented of their wicked ways and turned back to God, he blessed them by bringing healing and restoration to the land.

God is a God of restoration. That is one of the most powerful truths in Scripture. Whether it is a nation that has turned away from God, a soul who has lost their way to sin, or a marriage that is steeped in struggle and chaos, God is in the business of bringing healing and restoration. All we have to do is turn our hearts away from sin and selfishness and back toward his will and guidance.

Scripture says, "God opposes the proud but shows favor to the humble" (James 4:6). It took a lot of humility for Mike to humble himself before God and Kathy and confess his unfaithfulness. And it took an equal measure of humility for Kathy to accept his confession and stay with him. They both had to swallow a lot of pride and resentment to save their marriage. But they were willing to do that, and because of it, God was able to rebuild their strained relationship.

God can heal any marriage, no matter how fractured and disenfranchised it has become. He can restore any couple to the glory that they were meant to have. He did it for Mike and Kathy. He did it for Karen and me.

He can do the same for you.

Wherever you are in your relationship, let me encourage you to let God come in and make it the best it can possibly be. Whether your marriage is simply struggling through some difficult issues or teetering on the brink of divorce, God can bring restoration. He can do what you could never accomplish in your own power.

Don't allow your marriage to become another statistic. Don't let Satan tear apart what God has supernaturally joined together. Don't give up on the most sacred promise you've ever made.

Whatever it takes to stay true to your covenantal vows, commit today that you will do it.

Stay true to the journey, and let God worry about the destination. The result will be a passionate, lifelong love affair!

Eight-Week Study Guide
for Couples and Small Groups

One of the bellwether characteristics of most happily married couples is that they seek out other happily married couples to hang out with. They instinctively understand the importance of developing relationships with others who can hold them accountable and help make their marriages better. If you want a strong and vibrant marriage, you begin by attaching yourself to other great marriages.

One of the best ways I know of finding these types of healthy relationships is through joining a small group Bible study for couples. The following eight-week study guide is designed to help you do just that. If you're presently involved in a small group, perhaps you can suggest this study for your next session. If you're not in a small group, this is a great opportunity to start one. Whatever your situation, I hope you take advantage of this great resource.

Here's how the study works. Each lesson walks you through two chapters of the book, setting a manageable pace for reading. This should give you plenty of time to process the material as you read through the book. You'll get more out of the study if you read the chapters and then answer the questions before each meeting.

Each lesson also includes a section titled "For Couples Only." This is intended to be a private weekly exercise between you and your spouse. I strongly encourage you to set aside time each week to discuss these questions together and not overlook this part of the lesson. Communication is critical to building a strong marriage, so this is perhaps the most important part of the study.

Finally, I've included a weekly Scripture for meditation. As you pray about your marriage—both in private and with your spouse—I encourage you to meditate on this passage and listen to what God is saying to you regarding your relationship.

My prayer is that God will strengthen your marriage as you apply these biblical principles to your relationship, and that through God's grace, you will find the same joy and fulfillment in your marriage that Karen and I have been blessed to discover in ours.

Week 1

Chapter 1: Great Marriages Don't Just Happen

1. What was the most moving music concert you've ever attended? What is your reaction when you hear flawless music from a talented musician?

2. What is one skill that you've developed in your life? How would you describe the work it took to develop it?

3. We're encouraged when we see a couple still happily married after forty or fifty years of marriage. What is your first thought when you see couples like that?

4. Why do you think so many have bought into the "soul mate" myth?

5. It takes time and effort to develop a meaningful, lifelong love affair. What would you say are some of the most important skills couples need to have to grow a strong marriage?

6. As couples, most of us aren't satisfied with simply a good marriage; what we want is a *great* marriage. How would you define a good marriage? How is that different from a great marriage?

7. In many ways, marriage is like two rivers coming together and forming one dynamic river. In what ways is that true?

8. Do you agree that any marriage can have a 100 percent chance of success with the right tools and skills? Explain why.

9. What is the one concept or idea from this chapter that spoke to your heart the most?

Chapter 2: When Love Fails

1. How did you feel when you read the story of Walter and Lisa?

2. Do you know any similar stories of failed marriages and broken vows? If so, please share them, but do so in a way that protects the identities of those involved.

3. Why are couples under greater stress and temptation today than in years past?

4. In what ways is love like a garden? See how many analogies you can draw from that idea.

5. Why is it important in marriage for couples to understand the inherent differences between men and women? How do these differences cause conflict? How do they work to draw us even closer?

6. If you feel comfortable doing so, share some of the struggles you had in the early years of your marriage. Are any of these issues still weighing on your relationship?

7. Share what skills or insights you are hoping to gain from this study on marriage.

8. What is the one concept or idea from this chapter that spoke to your heart the most?

For Couples Only

1. If you don't already have a regularly scheduled date night, begin this week to make that a habit. Once a week would be ideal, but if that's not possible, you might start by going out twice a month. Pick a night that works for both of you and put it on your calendar.

2. During this week's date, talk about the story of Walter and Lisa. Discuss ways that you can work as a couple to make sure that what happened to them never happens in your marriage.

3. Talk to each other about your goals for this study, and share what you hope it will do to strengthen your marriage.

Scripture Meditation

Let us consider how we may spur one another on toward love and good deeds.

Hebrews 10:24–25

Week 2

Chapter 3: A Journey of Surrender

1. Begin this week by briefly sharing the story of your courtship and marriage. Tell how you first met. How did you feel toward your spouse during your first date?

2. When did you first realize that you wanted to spend the rest of your life with your mate?

3. Do you feel you had any unrealistic expectations when you first got married? If so, in what ways did these expectations create conflict during your first few years of marriage?

4. If you're comfortable doing so, share one struggle you've had in your marriage that you were able to resolve. What did you do to overcome this point of conflict?

5. What does it mean to surrender your marriage to God?

6. Have you ever had to surrender an issue or conflict to God to get past it? How hard was that to do? How did God work to bring your relationship through it?

7. Are there any issues or conflicts you need to surrender to God right now? If you would be willing to, please share them with the group.

8. What is the one concept or idea from this chapter that spoke to your heart the most?

Chapter 4: The Power of Covenant

1. What are some inherent problems that arise when you try to separate marriage from God?

2. The problem with secular counseling is that divorce is almost always presented as a viable option when couples can't seem to work through issues of conflict. What are some other dangerous ideas promoted by secular counseling?

3. Describe what it means to be "one flesh" (Gen. 2:24) in the eyes of God.

4. God formed every living creature from dust except for Eve. He created her from Adam's rib. Why did he do that? What are some of the implications we can draw from this truth?

5. Describe the difference between a covenant and a contract. In what ways is a covenantal relationship more binding and sacred than a contractual one?

6. How well did you understand the vows you were making on the day of your wedding? What do you know now that you wish you had understood then?

7. Why is it important to see your spouse as the one God created specifically with your needs and desires in mind? How does that truth change the way you relate to each other?

8. What does it mean to embrace God's larger story for your marriage?

9. What is the one concept or idea from this chapter that spoke to your heart the most?

For Couples Only

1. Spend time this week discussing areas of your marriage that you feel you have not surrendered to God. Pray with your spouse about these areas, and discuss what you need to do to fully give those things over to God's will.

2. Talk about what it means to you as a couple to take your marriage into the larger story with God. Discuss some concrete things you can do to allow God to be an integral partner in your marriage.

3. During your date night this week, reminisce about the first date you went on together. Try to remember where you went, what you did, and what each of you were wearing. Remind your spouse what it was that first attracted you to them.

Scripture Meditation

That is why a man leaves his father and mother and is united to his wife, and they become one flesh.

Genesis 2:24

Week 3

Chapter 5: God's Dream for Your Marriage

1. How would you answer the question, "Why did God create marriage?"

2. In what ways does marriage transcend the natural realm and lift us into the spiritual realm?

3. Read Ephesians 5:22–33. In your own words, explain how marriage is an analogy of Christ's relationship to the church. What is the "mystery" that Paul speaks of?

4. If marriage is an earthly demonstration of Christ's commitment to the church, what are the implications for couples? How does that change the way you view your spouse?

5. What would happen if all couples started seeing their relationship the way God sees it?

6. Has God ever given you a vision of his purpose for your life? How did he reveal that purpose? Have you seen his vision come to reality?

7. Share what you think God's vision is for your marriage.

8. What is the one concept or idea from this chapter that spoke to your heart the most?

Chapter 6: Meeting God on the Mountain

1. What do you think about the idea of an annual vision retreat? What are some things about it that you like and dislike? .

2. Why is communication so critical to a healthy marriage? What are some skills we all need to develop to be better communicators?

3. How would you describe your present level of communication with your spouse?

4. What are the areas of communication that you most need to work on?

5. There are primarily three types of communication in marriage—reactive, radioactive, and proactive. In your own words, describe the differences between these three.

6. How would you describe your primary method of communication?

7. If you were to plan a vision retreat with your spouse, where would you go? Share with the group your idea of a perfect vision retreat.

8. What is the one concept or idea from this chapter that spoke to your heart the most?

For Couples Only

1. This week, begin planning a vision retreat with your spouse. Discuss where you'd like to go and how many days you think

you could get away. If possible, set a date and begin making arrangements.

2. During this week, spend time each day praying about your vision retreat. Ask God to begin working in your hearts, preparing you for the event. Ask him to reveal any areas that you need to discuss during your vision retreat. Also, pray that he would pave the way for a productive and enjoyable time away.

3. Be ready to share with the group during your next meeting what you have planned regarding your vision retreat so they can be praying with you as you prepare to go.

Scripture Meditation

Again, truly I tell you that if two of you on earth agree about anything they ask for, it will be done for them by my Father in heaven. For where two or three gather in my name, there am I with them.

Matthew 18:19–20

Week 4

Chapter 7: The Language of Love

1. Have you ever had a frustrating experience at a store's customer service counter? Describe it to the group.

2. How did you feel about the store after that experience? Did the experience make you less likely to shop there? Have you been back since?

3. Have you ever had a positive experience in a retail store? Describe it to the group.

4. How do you usually react when your spouse comes to you with a concern or complaint? How *should* you react?

5. Explain why almost all arguments in marriage are caused by poor communication.

6. When was the last time you encouraged your spouse to come to you if they have any complaints or concerns about your marriage? Do you think they feel free to be honest with you? Why or why not?

7. Spend time discussing the five critical skills of effective communication outlined in this chapter. Talk about which skill

you feel you most need to work on, as well as which skills you feel are your strong suits.

8. What is the one concept or idea from this chapter that spoke to your heart the most?

Chapter 8: Great Marriages Run in Packs

1. Of all the close friends you've had as a couple, how many have been divorced?

2. Have you ever witnessed a friend or co-worker led astray through an ungodly relationship? Did you see it coming? Describe that experience to the group.

3. Why does peer pressure play such a huge role in our lives, even as we get older?

4. Have you ever cut ties with friends because you felt they were a bad influence? How did God honor that decision?

5. Why is it important for married couples to surround themselves with godly Christian couples? Describe some relationships that have helped mentor you in your marriage, making it stronger.

6. Do you feel that you have a close-knit group of friends that hold you accountable in your life and marriage? Discuss some of these friends and what they mean to you.

7. How careful are you and your spouse about the friends you allow into your inner circle of friends?

8. Discuss how your group can work to "spur one another on" (Heb. 10:24) and hold each other accountable.

9. What is the one concept or idea from this chapter that spoke to your heart the most?

For Couples Only

1. This week, spend some time talking about the level of communication in your marriage. Are you communicating as well as you should? Are there areas you need to work on? Does your spouse feel free to complain when they have a concern? Discuss ways that you need to be more open and honest with each other.

2. Discuss the five skills of effective communication together. Ask your spouse which areas you most need to work on. Pray together, asking God to help you learn better communication skills.

3. Spend some time discussing the close friends you have as a couple. Are there any friends dragging you down in your relationship? Do you think God wants you to cut ties with any of them? Discuss some of your healthy friendships, and pray that God would help draw you closer to those friends.

Scripture Meditation

Walk with the wise and become wise, for a companion of fools suffers harm.

Proverbs 13:20

Week 5

Chapter 9: The Gardener and the Cheerleader

1. Why is the high divorce rate such a critical problem in today's society?

2. Read Ephesians 5:21–33. Discuss why this is such a counter-cultural concept of marriage. What does it mean to "submit to one another out of reverence for Christ" (v. 21)?

3. Why do so many wives recoil at the thought of submitting to their husbands? Do you think we understand what God means when he tells women to submit? How would you define godly submission?

4. Spend some time discussing the Ephesians 5 model for marriage. Do you agree that it is God's "perfect plan for marriage"? Why or why not?

5. Husbands are commanded to love their wives "as Christ loved the church" (v. 25). What does that mean? What are some ways husbands can do that?

6. How does the Ephesians 5 model for marriage give couples the key to lifelong attraction? Have you experienced that truth

in your marriage? Give some concrete examples of how that model works.

7. How does the Ephesians 5 model release your spouse to reach their full potential?

8. How does the Ephesians 5 model disable our sin nature? Give some specific examples of that truth from your own marriage.

9. What is the one concept or idea from this chapter that spoke to your heart the most?

Chapter 10: Your Husband's Dream Wife

1. Husbands, have you ever talked to your wife about your marital needs? Is this an area that you can discuss freely with each other?

2. The four basic needs of men are respect, sex, friendship, and domestic support. Why do you think God created men with such universal needs?

3. How would you define godly submission? How is that different from being subservient?

4. Of the four basic needs of men, almost all husbands rate respect as their number one need. Husbands, would you say that is true for you? On a scale of 1 to 10, with 10 being the highest, how would you rate your need for respect from your spouse? Why?

5. Most men would say that sexual intimacy is one of their most important needs in marriage. Why is that true? Would you say

it is due to living in an overly sexualized society, or are men simply wired that way? Explain why you think that.

6. Why is it so important to a husband to be friends with his wife? What does that mean in real terms? What are some ways that a wife can work to meet this need?

7. Why is domestic support important to men? What barriers and distractions do women have to contend with in this area? How can wives work to meet this need?

8. Wives, describe what it means to have a servant spirit. Why is it important to meet not only your husband's needs but also his deepest desires?

9. What is the one concept or idea from this chapter that spoke to your heart the most?

For Couples Only

1. During your date night this week, instead of going to a movie, spend some time at a quiet location where you can sit and visit—maybe a coffee shop or a bakery. Discuss the concepts of a gardener and a cheerleader as described in chapter 9. Talk about what that means to each of you in concrete terms.

2. Wives, ask your husband about his four basic needs in marriage. Have him rate these needs in order of importance, then ask how well he feels you are meeting those needs. Encourage him to be open and honest with you. Promise that you won't get angry or defensive.

3. Wives, say to your husband, "I understand your needs, but what are your inmost desires?" Then commit to looking for opportunities to meet those desires.

Scripture Meditation

Wives, submit yourselves to your own husbands as you do to the Lord. For the husband is the head of the wife as Christ is the head of the church, his body, of which he is the Savior. Now as the church submits to Christ, so also wives should submit to their husbands in everything.

Ephesians 5:22–24

Week 6

Chapter 11: Your Wife's Dream Husband

1. Husbands, when was the last time you asked your wife if she was happy? Is that something you discuss often with her?

2. The four basic needs of women are security, nonsexual affection, open and honest communication, and leadership. Would you agree that these are universal needs among women? Why do you think God wired most women this way?

3. Paul says in his letter to the Corinthians that man "is the image and glory of God; but woman is the glory of man" (1 Cor. 11:7). What do you think that means? In concrete terms, describe what it means for wives to reflect their husband's glory.

4. In Ephesians 5, Paul tells husbands to "love their wives as their own bodies" (v. 28). Describe what Paul means by that. What are some ways a husband can obey this command?

5. The greatest need of most women in marriage is security. What does it mean to make a wife feel secure? What are some things husbands do to foster insecurity in their relationships? How can they guard against those things?

6. Women also need nonsexual affection in marriage. Wives, describe what that means in real terms. What are some things a husband can do to meet his wife's need in this area?

7. Open and honest communication is another critical need for women. Why is that so hard for most men? What can husbands do to better fulfill this need for their wives?

8. The fourth need of women is leadership. Describe what it means for husbands to lead their families. What are some examples of healthy leadership within marriage?

9. What is the one concept or idea from this chapter that spoke to your heart the most?

Chapter 12: Two Servants in Agape

1. This chapter begins with the story of Jimmy's uncle Charles, who wrote a poem for his wife every day of their marriage. Can you think of any similar stories from your own experience? Share them with the group.

2. Read through the five levels of fulfillment outlined in this chapter. Where would you place your marriage on that scale? Where would you like it to be?

3. How would you define a "servant spirit" marriage?

4. Do you agree that marriage is a skill and that any couple can develop that skill with the right tools and teaching? Explain why or why not.

5. Describe how agape love is different from the way most people would define *love*.

6. How does the knowledge of God's unconditional love strengthen your faith and deepen your love for God?

7. What does it mean to decide to love your spouse? What are some ways you can do that?

8. What is the one concept or idea from this chapter that spoke to your heart the most?

For Couples Only

1. During this week's date night, it's the wife's turn to talk about her needs. Visit the same coffee shop or bakery that you did last week, but this time, husbands, ask your wife about her basic needs in marriage. Have her rate her needs in order of importance.

2. Wives, talk to your husband about his role in meeting your basic needs. Be honest about your feelings. Is he meeting your four basic needs?

3. Husbands, ask your wife, "What do you need me to do better to make you feel more secure?" Commit to having an open mind and a receiving spirit as she answers. Then promise to begin looking for ways to better meet her needs and desires.

Scripture Meditation

Husbands, love your wives, just as Christ loved the church and gave himself up for her to make her holy, cleansing her by the washing with water through the word. . . . In this same way, husbands ought to love their wives as their own bodies.

Ephesians 5:25–26, 28

Week 7

Chapter 13: Dynamic Love

1. Read Revelation 2:2–5. What was the sin of the church at Ephesus? Discuss the reasons God had for threatening to remove his lampstand from their midst.

2. What do you think causes a church to lose its first love? Discuss some factors at work when that happens.

3. Why is it such an insult to God when Christians become lukewarm in their faith? What does it say about our faith? What does it say about God?

4. Have you ever experienced a lull in your relationship with God? What did you do to recapture the love you had lost?

5. Have you ever experienced a similar lull in your marriage relationship? What did you do to rekindle the spark?

6. Psalm 98:1 says, "Sing to the LORD a new song, for he has done marvelous things." What does it mean to sing a new song to God? Why is God glorified when we do that?

7. In what ways can you sing new songs in your marriage relationship?

8. What is the one concept or idea from this chapter that spoke to your heart the most?

Chapter 14: Fearless Love

1. Would you consider yourself a driven person? If so, what do you think causes you to push yourself to achieve?

2. Drivenness, at its core, is simply a need to control the world around us. What are some other damaging ways we work to maintain control of our lives?

3. Do you find yourself worrying more than you should? What are some of the things you worry about? Why do you think worry is such a destructive force?

4. What does worry do to your relationship with God? With your spouse? With others?

5. Why is fear the enemy of faith? What do our fears say to God?

6. If you're comfortable doing so, share with the group some of your greatest fears. How have these fears created conflict in your relationships? In your marriage?

7. In this chapter, we discussed the core fears of men and women. How do these fears work to damage your relationship with God? How do they work to cause conflict in your marriage relationship?

8. The most critical step in overcoming fear is to give your fears to God. Discuss some concrete ways to do that.

9. What is the one concept or idea from this chapter that spoke to your heart the most?

For Couples Only

1. Spend some time discussing the "temperature" of your marriage. Are there areas of your relationship that seem to have grown stale and boring? Have you found yourself falling into a rut? Take an honest look at this issue, and share your hearts openly with each other.

2. Discuss some things you can do as a couple to rekindle those areas that seem to be getting cold. What steps can you take to revitalize your relationship? What steps can you take to keep those areas from growing cold in the future?

3. Spend some time discussing your core fears. In what ways have these fears kept you from growing deeper in your relationship? What should you be doing as a couple to help alleviate these fears in the future?

Scripture Meditation

Love is patient, love is kind. It does not envy, it does not boast, it is not proud. It does not dishonor others, it is not self-seeking, it is not easily angered, it keeps no record of wrongs. Love does not delight in evil but rejoices with the truth. It always protects, always trusts, always hopes, always perseveres. Love never fails.

1 Corinthians 13:4–8

Week 8

Chapter 15: Covenantal Love

1. Do you agree that loyalty is in short supply these days? What are some factors that contribute to this dynamic? Do you find that you are less loyal to businesses than you once were?

2. In your own words, describe what it means to have a shopper's mentality.

3. How has this type of thinking worked to undermine marriages? Have you experienced this mentality among your peers or co-workers? How has it affected the relationships of people you know?

4. In what ways has humanistic philosophy infiltrated church theology? How has it affected our faith? How has it affected our relationships?

5. Marriage works only on the basis of covenant. Why is this true? What happens when this truth becomes lost and distorted?

6. Every covenant has three distinct components: a sacred oath, a sign and a seal, and a sacrifice. Discuss these three components one at a time. Why are they so critical to the covenantal bond?

7. Keeping covenant has never been more difficult than it is today. Why do you think that's true? What are some societal factors that make covenant keeping so difficult?

8. What are some things couples should do to keep their covenantal vows to each other?

9. What is the one concept or idea from this chapter that spoke to your heart the most?

Chapter 16: The Journey of Love

1. Do you agree that in God's economy, "the journey is the destination"? What does that mean?

2. Why is God so interested in seeing us develop healthy relationships? What do relationships bring into our lives that we otherwise might not have?

3. In what ways have you seen God work through your relationships to make you a stronger person? Discuss ways he has used others to mentor you in your life and faith.

4. Can you relate to Dr. Dobson's experience during his first time on the golf course? In what ways have you found yourself "chasing a little white ball" in life and completely losing sight of the beauty that surrounds you?

5. The longer you live, the more precious ordinary moments with your family become. What are some tender moments with your family that you treasure deeply? Is there a specific story or event you could share with the group?

6. In your own words, describe what it means to cleave to each other as a couple. Why is cleaving such an important biblical principle?

7. Discuss some of the ways you and your spouse work to keep from drifting apart as a couple.

8. What is the one concept or idea from this chapter that spoke to your heart the most?

9. To end this final lesson, take a few minutes to talk about what your spouse means to you. Tell them what you most love and appreciate about them. Reaffirm your commitment to the marriage. You can either break off in private or take turns sharing within the group.

For Couples Only

1. Now that the study is complete, take some time alone this week to write down the things God has been teaching you during the course of the study. What areas of your marriage have you felt convicted to work on? What does God want you to change about the ways in which you relate to your spouse and your children?

2. After journaling these thoughts, use this week's date night for one more quiet visit to your favorite coffee shop or bakery. Share your notes with your spouse. Tell them how God has been moving in your heart, what areas of the relationship you believe he wants you to work on, and how you plan to stay true to your commitment. Then allow your partner to share their notes as well.

3. Finally, agree with each other that you will continue your regular date nights in the future, making them a nonnegotiable part of your marriage. Commit also to annual vision retreats. These are two critical ingredients for developing a lifelong love affair.

Scripture Meditation

Dear children, let us not love with words or speech but with actions and in truth.

1 John 3:18

Jimmy Evans is founder and CEO of MarriageToday, a ministry based in Dallas, Texas, that is devoted to helping couples build strong and fulfilling marriages and families. Jimmy and his wife, Karen, are passionate about marriage. Together they cohost *MarriageToday with Jimmy and Karen*, a nationally syndicated television program broadcast weekly into over ninety million homes in America and more than two hundred countries worldwide.

Jimmy has served as the senior leader of Trinity Fellowship Church in Amarillo, Texas, for the past thirty years. During his years of leadership, Trinity has grown from nine hundred to over ten thousand members. He also serves as an apostolic elder of Gateway Church in Southlake, Texas; is an overseer of New Life Church in Colorado Springs, Colorado; and presides over the Trinity Fellowship Association of Churches, which oversees churches in five states.

Jimmy has authored more than ten books, among which are his popular works *Marriage on the Rock*, *Freedom from Your Past*, *7 Secrets of Successful Families*, and *Ten Steps Toward Christ*.

Jimmy and Karen have been married thirty-nine years and have two married children and four grandchildren.

Frank Martin is the author or co-author of nineteen books, including *Furious Pursuit* and *Embracing Eternity* (co-authored with Tim LaHaye and Jerry Jenkins). He is a frequent collaborator, having written books with numerous notables, including Nicky Cruz, Bill McCartney, Dr. O. S. Hawkins, and Wally Armstrong. He was also a contributing writer for the recently released *New NIV Men's Devotional Bible*.

Frank served eighteen years as a family commentary writer for Dr. James Dobson and Focus on the Family. He has been published in numerous magazines, including *Discipleship Journal*, *Marriage Partnership*, *Image*, *UpReach*, *Today's Child*, and *Pray!*

Frank and his wife, Ruthie, have been married for twenty-seven years. They currently reside in Colorado Springs, Colorado, with their two children, David and Kandilyn. For a more extensive bio, visit Frank's website at www.frankmmartin.com.

Rock Solid
PARTNERS

It's not often you get the opportunity to make your own life better while helping thousands of others at the same time. But you can do that right now by saying "yes" to becoming a Rock Solid Partner.

MarriageToday has spent years developing proven tools for healing the most shattered of relationships and for making good marriages truly great. When you say "yes" to joining the ranks of MarriageToday's Rock Solid Partners, you get the good feeling that comes from knowing you are having a powerful, positive impact on the lives of children and their parents.

You also get exclusive access to our monthly *Dream Marriage Library* resource—a bundle of topical help and insight that is already transforming relationships all over America.

MONTHLY DONATION OPTIONS

$14 month	$28 month	$56 month
DIGITAL LIBRARY ACCESS	MONTHLY DVDs IN THE MAIL	PARTNER PERKS

Sign up now by visiting
MARRIAGETODAY.COM/PARTNERS